India's Engagement with East Africa:

Opportunities and Challenges

India's Engagement with East Africa:

Opportunities and Challenges

by

Dr. Nivedita Ray

Vij Books India Pvt Ltd
New Delhi (India)

Indian Council of World Affairs
Sapru House, New Delhi

Published by

Vij Books India Pvt Ltd
(Publishers, Distributors & Importers)
2/19, Ansari Road
Delhi – 110 002
Phones: 91-11-43596460, 91-11-47340674
Fax: 91-11-47340674
e-mail: vijbooks@rediffmail.com
web : www.vijbooks.com

First Published in India in 2015

ISBN: 978-93-82652-94-6 (Hardback)
ISBN: 978-93-84464-36-3 (Paperback)

Paperback edition published in 2016

Contents

Acknowledgements

I am thankful to ICWA for encouraging the pursuit and preparation of this book project on *India's Engagement with East Africa: Opportunities and Challenges*. Foremost, I am grateful to the Director General, Ambassador Rajiv Kumar Bhatia for his encouragement and support to undertake the study. I am also sincerely appreciative of the support provided by ICWA Deputy Director General, Shri Narendra Saxena in accomplishing this project.

This book project is an academic enterprise to study and explore the existing trends and possible transformations in the India-East Africa engagement in different sectors, both from a bilateral as well as regional perspective. It discusses the opportunities and challenges present for India and the East African countries. The course of this project is based on research as well as interactions and discussions.

I owe much gratitude to Ambassador Sudhir Devare, Ambassador Sashank and Professor Ajay Dubey, for their valuable insights and suggestions during the conceptualisation of this book project. I am thankful to my colleagues in ICWA for having been a part of this academic exercise.

I am grateful to a number of international scholars whom I interacted with and in particular those whom I interviewed during my field study. My interactions with various experts, who participated in the ICWA India-Africa conferences, have also greatly benefited in improving this study. I would like to acknowledge the assistance given by the Indian missions in Tanzania and Uganda for the field work.

I thank the ICWA and JNU library, and the publication unit for their assistance and support. Last, but not the least, I thank my family for their constant support and understanding.

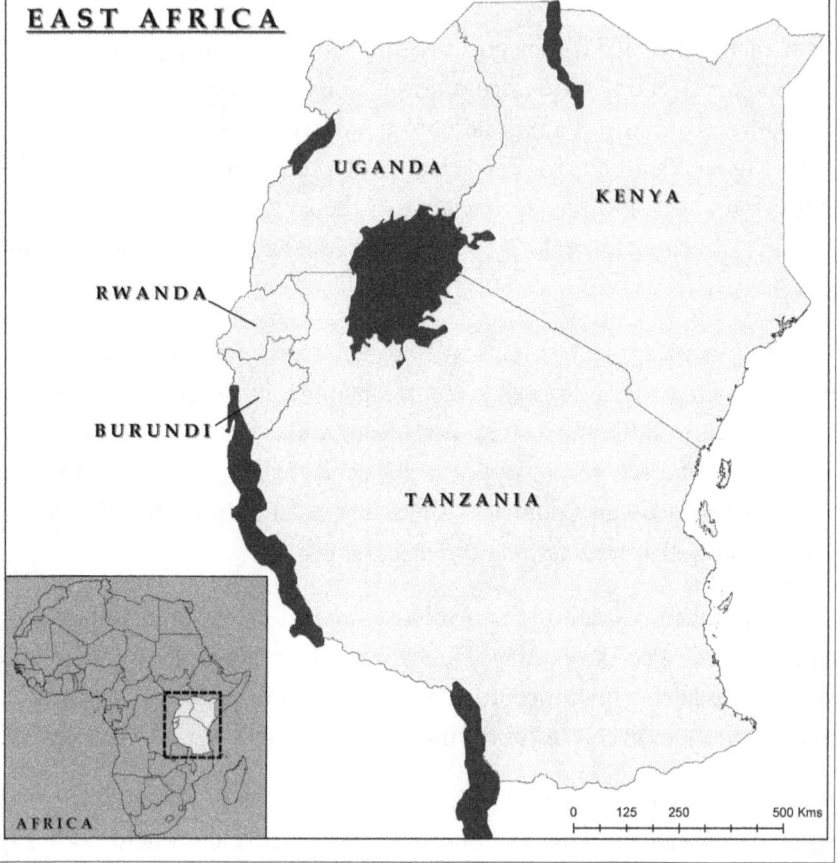

EAST AFRICA

UGANDA

KENYA

RWANDA

BURUNDI

TANZANIA

AFRICA

0   125   250   500 Kms

Introduction

Of Africa's five key regions, East Africa (EA) has enjoyed the oldest links with India. These links built through trade, commerce and travel across the Indian Ocean, dates back to antiquity. Geographical proximity and the Indian Ocean made people of both sides to know each other. Over the ensuing years these linkages have become more extensive. In the current decade, India has taken significant steps to strengthen and diversify cooperation with East Africa. The Delhi Declaration and Framework of Cooperation Agreement as well as the Addis Ababa declaration and the Framework of Enhanced Cooperation, signed between India and African countries in the India-Africa Forum Summit, held in April 2008 and 2011 respectively provide a structure for establishing a long-term, stable partnership based on equality and mutual benefit. As part of this process, India's engagement with East Africa has acquired a greater momentum and expansion.

East Africa as a region is variously defined, but for the purpose of this book East Africa refers to the East African Community (EAC) comprising Kenya, Tanzania, Uganda, Rwanda, and Burundi. For India this region assumes immense significance both at the bilateral and regional level. Being the world's new growth pole with a market of some 300 million people and most importantly with the recent oil discoveries East Africa has become an economically vibrant region of Africa. It comprises of resource potential countries – with minerals, oil and fertile land (Uganda and oil-rich Kenya for instance is replete with mineral resources such as uranium and diamonds, 20 percent land had been exploited for farming). Further, the location of the region falls under India's strategic maritime neighborhood. For tackling problems like piracy and terrorism in the Indian Ocean region India needs to work with the region both bilaterally and regionally. The large affluent Indian diaspora in East Africa – a heritage resource - makes this region as a natural partner for India in terms of the people to people linkages.

For the East African countries, India is a source of the low-cost, adaptable and affordable technologies, and expertise on agricultural development, water resource irrigation, telecommunications, pharmaceuticals, human resource development, and military capability.

There is growing complementarities of interests between both the regions in terms of Africa's developmental needs and India's strengths. Based on the larger framework of cooperation between India and Africa, both sides are currently pursuing a partnership model of engagement, wherein the focus has been on economic, social and security sector. It centers on trade, private sector investment, aid, capacity building, diaspora resources and security challenges. The approach that India has adopted has been development-centric and India's attractiveness as an alternative development partner in the region is now being widely noted. The partnership model of engagement is claimed to be different from others as it is request based and is one seeking mutual benefit through a consultative process.

Both are moving forward with plans and strategies to deepen their engagement. As this engagement today is not only fast moving but also intense, it is important to reflect upon, how India's relations with the region have expanded since the first Summit in New Delhi in April 2008 in different sectors, and critically examine the opportunities and concerns. There is a need to scrutinize the partnership model of relationship between India and East African countries, to assess whether this partnership is sustainable in the longer term and; whether a balance is maintained between India's interest and priorities and expectations of East African countries?

It is important to evaluate the emerging areas of cooperation and examine whether India's approach is different vis-à-vis others? India has tremendous goodwill but has it been able to truly capitalize the full potential of its goodwill? What are the areas that India needs to focus on? While seizing opportunities in East Africa, is India mindful and sensitive to East Africa's concerns? India's footprint in Africa in general and East Africa in particular has been private-sector-led with limited diplomatic presence although it is picking up. As India's commercial interactions deepens with East Africa, and as it emerges to play a greater role in shaping the multilateral polity and global economy, would it be able to strike a balance between the South–South cooperation promoted by its policymakers and its interest? Would India's current involvement in East Africa work in the interests of the people in East Africa?

This book is primarily a macro level study, critically examining India's involvement in East Africa in various sectors, in the changing geopolitics of the region. It is motivated by the observations that India's rise as an economic and knowledge power and emergence as a key global player has been associated with robust and increasing intensification of its relations with African countries including East Africa and that these relationships are associated with both opportunities and concerns for East African countries as well as India. The primary purpose of this book is to present a comprehensive analysis of the key features and patterns of the current "partnership framework" engagement of India with East African countries in different sectors as a basis for achieving a fuller understanding of the impact of the framework of engagement and the development prospects of East African countries.

Efforts have been also made to emphasize and focus upon the contemporary relationship, which has seen discernible change, starting from India - Africa Forum summit in 2008, wherein the shared ideologies of anti-colonialism, anti-racialism, non-alignment no more remain the rallying points. How new drivers, priorities and imperatives and complementarities of interest are allowing both sides to enter into a "partnership" model of engagement has been explored. Further an analysis has been made about the patterns and form of engagement, the areas of convergences, the opportunities for cooperation and the concerns/ challenges as to whether mutuality of interest is served, and East African expectations are met.

The book aims to critically review India's current framework of engagement with East Africa and map the developments. It evaluates the changing contours of the contemporary India East Africa relations. Further it tries to explore India's opportunities in East Africa and assess East African needs and concerns in various sectors, such as human resource development, Trade and Investment, diaspora potential and Security.

Chapter one *India and East Africa Partnership: Historical Experiences and Current Realities* discusses the geo strategic significance of East African region and its importance to external players, and examines India and

East Africa engagement within the framework of India -Africa historical relations- pre-colonial, colonial, post-colonial. It explores East Africa's ancient links with India - dating 2000 yrs. back- through navigable Indian Ocean, establishment of trade and commerce, exchange of goods, people – to- people linkages (free voluntary movement), PIO linkages build through colonial needs and preferences (worked on the railways), and post-colonial linkages of shared ideologies of anti –colonialism , anti- racialism and non-alignment. Current partnership engagement- is examined against the historical backdrop with focus on the nature and pattern, development needs and capacity building, private sector led economic linkages, Indian diaspora and peace and security.

In Chapter two on *India and East Africa: Development Cooperation.* India's development assistance to East Africa is discussed with respect to infrastructure projects, institutional building, training programmes, and lines of credit offered for implementing project. In this chapter the India' development assistance policy is examined in terms of review of disbursement and impact of the assistance. The impact of development assistance in the region, with focus on question as to whether Indian pattern of assistance is different, has been noted. It also discusses the capacity building initiatives for human resource development and how it is being undertaken through different programmes and LoCs. There are concerns relating to implementation of projects, and its impact in terms of benefit to local people and Indians, which is also examined.

The *Role of Indian Private Sector in Economic Linkages* is the third chapter which examines the challenges and identifies new areas of cooperation in various sectors such as pharmaceuticals, agricultural development and Information and Communication Technology at the bilateral level and regional level.

Chapter four on *Indian Diaspora as Heritage Resource* draws on historical linkages – dissociation and association along with role, status and unique distinction of Indian Diaspora, It also examines the potential of Indian diaspora in promoting bilateral relations and economic engagements. It also studies the alignment of India's diaspora policy with India's Africa Policy and its immense potential for enhancing bilateral ties and promoting economic engagement.

Chapter five on *India and East Africa: Peace and Security Cooperation* discusses among others the maritime security concerns, terrorism, impact of security in the economic stability in the region and measures and mechanisms of regional cooperation.

The last chapter *Conclusion* sums up the opportunities and concerns pertaining to India's current engagement with East Africa.

Chapter - 1

India and East Africa Partnership: Historical Experiences and Current Realities

India's relations with East African countries is multidimensional and rests on firm historical foundations of shared colonial past and similarity of post-Independence development experience. Over the years the relationship has evolved and has become more extensive. From an ideologically driven relationship based on shared commitments of anti-colonialism, anti-racialism, Non-aligned Movement (NAM) and Afro-Asian solidarity, it has moved into a more pragmatic engagement with focus on economic and geo-strategic issues. Particularly after the 2008 India-Africa Summit there has been a perceptible shift in the relations with the countries in the region with renewed initiatives taken by India. Significant steps have been taken to strengthen and diversify cooperation with East Africa at the bilateral and regional level. The Framework of Cooperation agreement signed between India and African countries in both the India-Africa Forum Summits, held in April 2008 and May 2011, provides a framework for the cooperation in various sectors.

The region assumes immense strategic significance for India and vice versa. It is the common interests that are driving this partnership. For India the main drivers have been a varied combination of inter-related political, strategic and economic factors related to its national and international ambitions. It claims the partnership to be in the true spirit of South – South cooperation, which is expected to grow stronger in the days to come. The approach adopted by India is development-centric focusing on empowerment, sustainable development, nurturing of human resource and peace and security of the region. This chapter will dwell on the expanding ties of India and East Africa in the current times and explore the factors that are shaping the relationship, as well as focus on the emerging areas of strategic interests and the challenges. The first section will deal on the historical perspective of India - East Africa ties in the backdrop of an overview of the region, emerging geopolitics contextualizing India, followed by current forms of bilateral engagement and the emerging trends and challenges.

Overview of the East African Region

To study India's engagement with the East African region, at the outset it is essential to have an understanding of the region and the emerging geopolitics. In this context therefore an overview of the region is significant. East Africa or Eastern Africa is variably defined by geography or geopolitics. Due to colonial territories of the British East Africa Protectorate and German East Africa, the term *East Africa* is often (especially in the English language) used to specifically refer to the area now comprising the three countries of Kenya, Tanzania and Uganda. However, this has never been the convention in many other languages, where the term generally had a wider, strictly geographic context and therefore typically included Djibouti, Eritrea, Ethiopia, Somalia and Sudan.[1] East Africa is often used broadly to refer to the area now comprising the countries of Kenya, Tanzania, Uganda, Rwanda and Burundi and (in a wider sense) also Somalia, Djibouti, Ethiopia, Eritrea, and South Sudan. But, in this study, the east African region only includes the countries in East African Community (EAC), which are Kenya, Tanzania, Uganda, Rwanda and Burundi. In East Africa, most countries in the region are on a solid growth path of between around 5 and 7 percent during the period 2012-2013, such as Rwanda, Tanzania, Ethiopia and Uganda. With the assumption of no major post-election turmoil in Kenya, growth is expected to amount to 4.5 percent in 2013 and to accelerate to above 5 percent in 2014. In 2012, GDP contracted and for 2013 only moderate growth is projected and some acceleration in 2014.

As regards to countries Kenya acts as a regional hub for trade and finance in East Africa. It is an important player in East and Central Africa. Strategically placed, with a major port, Mombasa, and well-developed financial markets, the country has the makings of a regional services hub in banking, information and transportation. The country's membership in the East African Community (with Tanzania and Uganda) and the Common Market for Eastern and Southern Africa (COMESA) makes it an attractive base for foreign investors and companies looking to access the East and Central African market. Through Kenya, an investor can access the COMESA market with over 380 million people[2]. Kenya has its fair share of internal and external challenges. For a long time it has been a stable and secure country in the region, still it has a long way to go to ensure the permanence of these issues. Externally it is now involved knee deep in the Somalia conflict which was spilling over into the northern part of the country. This has of course left the country exposed to attacks from Al Shabaab and its supporters. Internally, it still faces major identity issues inherited from the colonial era. This was especially clear in the aftermath of the 2007 elections; however Kenya has made several changes since then including hanging its constitution in the hopes that there will no repetitions of the past.

Tanzania is also relatively stable in the Eastern Africa region, although recently it has witnessed some religious tensions. After Somalia, which has been destroyed, Tanzania has the longest shoreline on the Indian Ocean. Zanzibar is a strategic island and the mainland is the only land mass which connects the Indian Ocean with Central Africa (the Democratic Republic of Congo). The country is rich in natural resources, including oil, uranium and gas. Due to its location it is emerging as an important factor in the security and geo-strategic environment of the Indian Ocean. The United States and China are increasing their presence in the recent years, Obama's visit, three months after a similar one by his Chinese counterpart; Mr Xi Jinping speaks volumes about the importance of the country. India attaches a lot of value to this country, which is evident from the Prime Minister choosing to visit Tanzania just after the 2011 summit held at Addis Ababa. Tanzania though remains one of the poorest countries in the world, with many of its people living below the World Bank poverty line, it has had some success in wooing donors and investors. Its annual growth rate has averaged 6.7 percent since 2006, one of the best in sub-Sahara Africa. One of the key areas of policy focus of the government has been promotion of sustained and shared economic growth. Dar es Salaam is the commercial capital and major sea port for Tanzania Mainland and it serves neighbouring land-locked countries of Malawi, Zambia, Burundi, Rwanda, and Uganda, as well as Eastern DRC. Other sea ports include Zanzibar, Tanga, and Mtwara. Because of its geographical and locational advantage, Dar es Salaam Port presents itself as the gateway into East and Central Africa. Furthermore, this renders Tanzania as a logical investment destination for investors. Moreover with attributes, such as its vast natural resources base, geographical and locational advantage, a large domestic market and a labour force, Tanzania is an ideal investment destination.

Unlike Kenya and Tanzania, Uganda is a landlocked country that has witnessed chronic political instability and erratic economic management, which produced a record of persistent economic decline that has left Uganda among the world's poorest and least-developed countries. The national energy needs have historically been more than domestic energy generation, though large petroleum reserves have been found in the west. However, endowed with significant natural resources, including ample fertile land, regular rainfall, and mineral deposits, it is thought that Uganda could feed all of Africa if it was commercially farmed. The economy of Uganda has great potential, and it appeared poised for rapid economic growth and development. Post Museveni period i.e. since 1986, the government has subsequently began implementing economic policies designed to restore price stability and sustainable balance of payments, improve capacity utilization, rehabilitate infrastructure, restore producer incentives through proper price policies, and improve resource mobilization and allocation in the public sector. The country has lot of investment potential particularly in the sector of agriculture and energy. In fact in the coming years energy sector will be the most dominant one, attracting investments and contributing to development of the region, provided the country take prudent policy measures towards such ends.

Rwanda is a landlocked country like Uganda. Seventeen years after the 1994 civil war and genocide, Rwanda is apparently stable, posting consistently strong economic growth rates and managing the country's considerable development assistance revenues effectively and transparently. Crime rates are low, the capital Kigali is remarkable for its orderliness, and the government's expressed vision of national reconciliation through development and service delivery has won accolades from the international community.[3] It has gone through many positive developments despite its turbulent history. For example, women have entered Rwanda's political and administrative institutions in impressive percentages. Politically it is very stable country, with well functioning institutions and rule of law and zero tolerance for corruption. It has sustained high economic growth rate of average 7.1 year after year since 2004 with stable inflation and exchange rate. Its investment climate is very friendly and a most competitive place in East Africa to do business. Its economy is primarily agrarian. Agriculture employs almost 80 percent of the population, accounting for more than 40 percent of gross domestic product (GDP) and more than 70 percent of exports. It is a hub for rapidly integrating East Africa as it is located centrally bordering three countries in East Africa, which has an existing custom union and common market since 2010 for 550 million people. Its potential areas of investment have been infrastructure, agriculture and energy.[4]

Like Rwanda, following a decade of conflict, Burundi has embarked upon an ambitious programme of political stabilization, national reconciliation and economic reforms. It is steadily emerging from a deep socio-political crisis that has destroyed its means of production. Although foreign direct investment (FDI) inflows are still very limited, conditions to attract higher levels are gradually put in place and opportunities are materializing. FDI attraction is now part of Burundi's development strategy, as exemplified by the recent creation of an investment promotion agency. The economy has grown an average 4 percent a year since 2005 but is still fragile because of its dependence on the primary sector, which is a major part of gross domestic product (GDP) and a big source of jobs. The government continued to pursue structural and financial reforms in order to strengthen the productive base, improve the business climate and revive economic activity. Burundi has abundant natural resources, especially minerals and hydro-electric potential, the development of which could substantially boost economic growth and job-creation.[5] For now, the mining sector is characterized by the expansion of subsistence mining by individuals that has limited economic benefits. From a sectoral perspective, almost a third of the GDP is generated by agricultural production alone (27.1 percent), followed by public services (25.6 percent), manufacturing and handicrafts (12.2 percent), and transport and communication (5.4 percent). Agriculture also accounts for about 60 percent of exports. This situation is a result of the long civil war and a lack of basic infrastructure, especially energy. The current political stability and the improved financial management contribute to Burundi's improved economic performance. In its role as a regional trading hub, Bujumbura should benefit from continued stability. As well, further integration with the EAC will support growth in the wholesale and retail sectors.[6] The integration of Burundi in the Eastern African Community (EAC) and in the Common Market for Eastern and Southern Africa (COMESA) represents an opportunity in terms of direct foreign investment. The EAC increases the size of the market accessible to Burundian products and stimulates the diversification of local production. On the other hand, the country will be the focal point of the trade within the region as it links up the central Africa, the oriental Africa and the southern Africa. Burundi could represent a strategic position for foreign investors wishing to invest in the region and to penetrate neighbouring markets. The opportunities and challenges currently facing Burundi are strongly linked to regional integration that forecast the creation of new realities for the direct foreign investments in the country.[7]

East African Community (EAC) which includes the above countries, Kenya, Uganda, Tanzania, Rwanda and Burundi, is one of the most integrated regional economic communities in Africa with a population of 133.5 million people, a combined GDP of 74.5 billion USD and a land area of 1.82 million sq. km. The realization of this regional economic bloc bears great strategic and geopolitical significance and prospects of a renewed and reinvigorated East African Community. The EAC aims at widening and deepening co–operation among the member countries in, among others, political, economic and social fields for their mutual benefit. To this extent the EAC countries established a Customs Union in 2005 and launched a Common Market in 2010, and are working towards the establishment of a Monetary Union and ultimately a Political Federation of the East African States. The regional integration process is at a high pitch at the moment as reflected by the encouraging progress of the East African Customs Union, with the signing in November 2009 and ratification in 2010 of the Common Market Protocol by all the Partner States. The negotiations for the East African Monetary Union, which commenced in 2011, and fast tracking the process towards East African Federation all underscore the serious determination of the East African leadership and citizens to construct a powerful and sustainable East African economic and political bloc.[8]

East African Geopolitics: Indian Context

Geo-politics, is the exercise of power over space that may not necessarily be one's own. The key thing in geopolitics is the ability to manipulate space to achieve political ends.[9] The east African region, for its strategic location with the Nile on the west, the red sea in the north and the Indian Ocean in the east, continues to be a point of interest locally and from extra continental forces. Since pre-colonial and colonial times East Africa has been engaged by several countries, and power blocks. As East African countries are growing economically at constant rate and have stabilized its political system under regional and continental cooperative framework, they are now trying to exercise their preference to divert and diversify the engagement from legacies of exploitation and subjugation. East Africa, no more is a marginalized player in the global affairs. The resource rich region has become the new chessboard for powers that shape global geopolitics.[10] It is East Africa which is setting the direction and pace of external power engagement, which it was unable to do earlier.

In this process non-colonizing countries and groups too are engaging East Africa, though differently, from colonial and super powers of cold war era. India, China and developing countries group have legacies, plans and priorities which intends to distinguish its relations from North-South or masters-colony pattern and they are increasingly becoming important partners for East African countries. With thus many players competing for political space and influence in the region, Eastern African countries are trying to identify their development cooperation priorities and regional security interests. The challenge is that politics of the west and eastern countries have the potential to divide the region, which is in dire need of peace, security and stability to forge ahead for the development and upliftment of the people's living standards.

The region has currently emerged as a real litmus test for existing and emerging powers of the World. Owing to its proximity with Asian continent, rise of Asian countries has obvious implications for the region. If current trade patterns are any indication, China and India have emerged as major trading partners to this region. In particular, China's economic and strategic engagements with the region have been commendable. Moreover, in the era of globalization led economic interdependence, securing Sea-Lanes of Communications (SLOCs) has become one of the major concerns for nation-states. Protection and security of existing and evolving SLOCs are intrinsically linked with secure and peaceful Asia, as most of the important SLOCs are located in the vicinity of the region.

The region has equally been important for the Western powers given the rise of Islamic forces, insecurity in the Indian Ocean, and discovery of new energy deposits. The United Kingdom has a military base in Kenya and the US is key military partner, while countries like France, Canada and Spain are heavily involved in humanitarian aid. The US also considers this region to be economically very significant. In the recent Obama visit to Tanzania, the US has announced a new venture, dubbed "Trade Africa," that aims to increase the flow of goods between the U.S. and sub-Saharan Africa. The initial phase will focus on East Africa - Burundi,

Kenya, Rwanda, Uganda and Tanzania - and aim to increase the region's exports to the U.S. by 40 percent.[11] China, the strong player in the region, which has invested a lot of resources in building infrastructure, in return it is continually growing as a trade partner of all these countries. India's engagement needs to be contextualized within the engagements of these powers in the region. All the external players in the region are competing for strategic interests and are trying to also influence the socio-economic and power politics in the region.

Significance of East Africa to India

India is also one of the powers which is leading a new push into East Africa. New imperatives and winds of change in both the territories add a fresh momentum to the engagement. There has been a rise in the significance of East Africa for India from an economic, political and security perspective. The positive changes seen in East Africa both politically and economically is one major factor that adds to the region's significance for India. The indicators of such change are very much evident. All East African countries have embraced multi-party democracy. Regular elections have become a common feature in the region.[12] Governance and transparency issues as well those of corruption are being taken up in a serious manner. There is greater consciousness now to put their own house in order and confidence to find own solutions for their own problems. In the international level the region is now playing an enhanced role. Economically the region is fast growing. Not only was the growth widespread across the countries in the region, it was also broad based, with many sectors contributing resources, finance, retail, agriculture, transportation and telecommunications.[13]

In the region there is immense goodwill owing to its historical and political solidarity with the countries in East Africa, unlike many other players, particularly the Asian actors like China. The Indian diaspora presence in the region adds to the friendly and close relations of India with East Africa. The Indian diaspora in the East African region has played a very significant role in India-East Africa relations. With their business ties with India and a good knowledge of Africa, Indians in East Africa have played a significant role in attracting new investments from India to the region. This diasporic connection makes this region special.

From an economic perspective, East Africa, unlike in the past has become a major trading destination. Trade and investment is one of the major drivers of current engagement. India's bilateral trade and investment in East African countries have reached significant proportions. In fact, in recent years, India's economic partnership with East African countries has been vibrant, extending beyond trade and investment to technology transfers, knowledge sharing, and skills development. The influx of Indian aid, capital and personnel also had potentially profound developmental consequences for the numerous East African countries. The Indian private sectors with its 'outward-looking' attitude, tempted by the easy availability of capital and driven by the search for new markets, have been targeting the countries in East Africa. The economic boom in India and the success of both home-grown and NRI/PIO (Non-Resident Indian/Person of Indian Origin) companies in Europe and parts of South America have provided Indian businesses the confidence to venture into African general and East Africa in particular. Moreover there is a growing recognition that East African economies are at a stage of development where India could offer the most appropriate technologies and products at competitive price. The success of India- Africa project partnership conclaves since 2005 indicates the growing interest of Indian industry in East Africa. The recent robust trends in Indo-East African trade relations, wherein bilateral trade has increased almost five fold in the last five years, makes it evident how East Africa is turning out to be an attractive destination for Indian private companies. Africa's share of India's global trade has also increased from 5.8 percent in 2002-2003 to 8 percent in 2006-2007[14]. Increased activities of Indian companies in East Africa have spurred the government to link its economic diplomacy in the continent more explicitly to its economic requirements.

From a geo-strategic perspective, East Africa's abundance energy resources has recently attracted India's attention like other players. In days to come it could be one of key drivers of India's relations with East Africa. India's growing energy needs have forced it to diversify its oil imports and look towards Africa, in a way to decrease its dependency on West Asian countries for its oil imports, which accounts for two third of the oil imports.[15] In recent years India is increasingly engaging with African oil-producing countries, namely Nigeria, Sudan, Côte d'Ivoire, Equatorial Guinea, Ghana, and Angola. Consequently, Africa accounts for about 20 percent of India's total import of mineral fuels. Other key African partners include South Africa, Egypt, Morocco, Tunisia and East African countries like Tanzania.[16]

East Africa region, which was never in the radar of international oil and gas industry, is now fast emerging as one of the hot zone for oil and gas exploration. With the recent massive discoveries in Uganda, Kenya, Somalia, Tanzania and Mozambique, the region has been drawing oil companies from around the world including Indian oil companies, which have made inroads into the gas sector in Tanzania and Mozambique. Experts say that East African oil may soon beat Middle Eastern oil in the global market. This is evident from the way these countries have been steadily defining their oil and gas reserves and demonstrating their willingness to work with foreign companies. The region is currently being projected as the growth engine for Africa's natural oil and gas sector. Its hydrocarbon resources seem to have the potential to stimulate economic growth both locally and regionally. For India and other players whose energy demand is growing, the fresh discoveries in these East African countries bring much hope. However, amidst all this enthusiasm it is important to assess how real the opportunities are and what are the hurdles that the region and the interested oil companies need to overcome to reap the benefits.

Undoubtedly the investment opportunities in the region are immense. Analysts say that East African region is home to at least 28 billion barrels of recoverable oil, 440 trillion cubic feet of gas and 14 billion barrels of natural gas liquids. It is projected that total oil production in the region (excluding Sudan) could reach approximately 210,000 barrels per day (bpd) in 2015, and nearly 389,000 bpd by 2020. In Uganda, Tullow Oil estimates oil reserves of approximately 2.4 billion barrels in Lake Albert Basin. About Kenya prospectors are increasingly confident that it could be the next big thing in oil and gas — experts say the geological profile of Kenya's northern Rift Valley is similar to that of Uganda's Lake Albert basin. Further north in Somali Puntland, two exploration wells have been already drilled and the initial results have been encouraging. All of Somalia and its offshore may become attractive once the security and political situation normalizes. Companies have also started prospecting for oil in Ethiopia, Democratic Republic of Congo and Eritrea. Industry leaders opine that East Africa is the new West Africa in terms of oil exploration. But while the oil discoveries look promising, it is gas that is causing the most excitement. The entire East Africa Rift System (EARS) and region, as well as the Indian Ocean coastline of Tanzania and Mozambique are highly prospective in gas. The gas discoveries are estimated to stand at more than 100 trillion cubic feet (tcf). Mozambique's has potential recoverable reserves of 30 trillion cu ft. Tanzania has approx. 7.5 billion cubic feet of gas reserves, with 70 million cubic feet /day capacity. Ethiopia's Ogaden basin –has an estimated reserve of 4 tcf of gas. It's not just the geology that makes East Africa so exciting – it's also the geography. East Africa's hydrocarbon resources face the lucrative markets of India and the Far East.

Exploiting these resources in East Africa is not without its challenges. The most significant challenges relate to poor infrastructure and political risks. Huge investment is required to build pipelines, refineries, LNG plants, roads and office buildings. The political risk challenges are also immense, such as corruption, weak regulatory mechanisms, competing political interests, and threat of being afflicted with resource curse, which is witnessed in many African countries having abundant natural resources. However, challenging environments are part and parcel of oil and gas exploration frontier and those need to be overcome to reap the benefits.

To overcome the hurdles of infrastructure, the East African countries are gradually recognizing the need to work together, so that they avoid unnecessary competition and find out common approach to reduce the cost. Some ideas such as, a centrally located major refinery facility and one international pipeline having different channels have been shared by various stakeholders in the region. Besides the infrastructure challenges to minimize the political risk, the countries are taking measures to have energy regulatory bodies and management policies aiming at ensuring equitable distribution of oil revenues, while taking into account the interests of the communities in oil-producing regions.

There is little doubt that East Africa is well on its way to becoming a major new oil and gas exporting territory. If the current obstacles are surmounted it will become a major global focus with far reaching consequences for the region. The rush has already begun. At the moment there is a mix of independents and medium-sized oil companies. But soon in the coming years there will be a different picture. For countries like India and China the geography of this region looks certainly more attractive, because the transportation routes to Asia is much easier compared with Middle East, where tankers have to go through choke points at the Strait of Hormuz. Indian companies like Bharat Petroleum and Videocon have already made inroads into the gas sector in Mozambique. But at present challenges are huge. No more its easy oil or gas for the Indian companies. So the question is will Indian companies be able to deal with these problems. But then one would also argue that they don't have much choice otherwise. With India's home production coming down and India's energy demand growing, India cannot afford to ignore the hydrocarbon potential of the region.

From India's security and strategic point of view there is a growing recognition that the eastern coast of Africa from South Africa to Somalia – fall under India's maritime strategic neighbourhood. Insecurity in the Indian Ocean region is on the rise, owing to the threat of terrorism, trans-national crime such as trafficking in drugs, arms and humans, and piracy. Alarming increase in incidents of piracy in Somali waters in particular threatens the security of the Sea Lanes of Communications (SLOCs) and impact global maritime trade, a large part of which passes through the Gulf of Aden. The Indian Navy particularly its Coast Guard has been active in its diplomacy in the Indian Ocean, providing maritime security cover. But despite all the measures that have been taken to curtail this menace the situation as termed by India is still "worrisome". While significant gains have been made in the last one year by the African Union Mission in Somalia (AMISOM) and Kenyan and Ethiopian forces in securing Mogadishu and other areas in south and central Somalia, terror group Al Shabaab with its recent affiliation to Al Qaeda remains a serious threat to peace and stability in Somalia and the larger region. India, which made an $2 million contribution in 2011 to the African Union and UN Trust Funds for AMISOM, is ready to provide further support to AMISOM.[17] As peace and stability of the region is of utmost importance to the region as well as to India's interest it.

Politically India has acknowledged the importance of African countries in global governance. In the context of UN reforms Africa is significant as it is rich in votes at the UN General Assembly. As India intensifies its efforts to bring about UN reform and secure for itself a permanent seat in the Security Council, the 53 votes from Africa in the General Assembly will play a crucial role.

East Africa's Development: India an Attractive Partner

For East Africa India holds immense significance from the perspective of its development and growth. India has been warmly welcomed to the region amid emerging shifts in attitudes towards the western worlds on the part of a growing proportion of East Africans. This entrancements with the poor track report with the western developments over the past fifty years, the double standards that western government practice in their relations with East African States and the tendency to give aids with one hand and to retrieve it from East African countries with the other through unfair trade practices, capital flight and depth structures, has generated a lot of debate among the east Africans over the past decades and has served as a rallying point for pursuing an alternative and independent East African Development Agenda[18]. From an East African perspective, the emergence of India as potentially important development partner came at this critical juncture when East African themselves were engaged in a major soul searching exercise to find out what is wrong with their development in the past half century. India's historical experiences as a former colony, and its spectacular development experience since the mid 1970s, have raised hopes among East African nations that they to can one day break away from the shackles of poverty, underdevelopment and aid dependency.[19]

Equally important is the demonstration effect of India's own development experiences to East African countries. Heavy investments in infrastructure, education, research and development (as opposed to the deflationary and austerity measures demanded by the Bretton Woods Institutions) were complemented with adjustable policies designed to enhance the competitiveness of the local producers through technological retooling and worker's retraining, than regulating the markets accordingly. These factors have helped rekindle interests within East Africa in the role of developmental states and the importance of experimenting with heterodox economic policies in order to successfully navigate the cold currents of economic globalizations, as India has done successfully.

There is also a growing vie that East African countries can learn a lot from Indian economic reform programmes of the past 30 years.

What East Africa needs, is external support for trade over aid - coupled with internal reforms. What East Africans want is partnerships and not exploitation. They need help in bringing transparency in institutions and governance in Africa. India stands relevant in sharing experiences and knowledge of e-governance, functioning of its financial institutions, conducting elections using electronic voting machines and ideas like financial inclusion, telemedicine and tele-education.

India is held in high esteem – in particular, on account of resilience of its democratic institutions and the manner and speed of its economic growth. As a democratic developing country, it serves as a role model for these African countries and is a source of support in various sectors, especially agriculture, services and small and medium scale manufacturing. Above all, it is the image of India – that of a leader in the information technology industry and computer software, biotechnology and telecommunications – that attracts Africa to India. East African countries have been interested in acquiring cost effective and intermediate technology from India. They have expressed special interest in forging partnership in areas such as Information Technology, agriculture, health and pharmaceuticals. Only half a million Africans have access to the internet, and there is thus a pressing need to narrow the "digital divide". East African countries want to benefit from India's prowess in the field of IT. East African leaders often quote the example of India's green revolution and its attainment of self sufficiency in food production. India's expertise in this sector can help to develop the African potential. The growing spread of diseases such as malaria, tuberculosis and HIV/AIDS have made health an important agenda for most African governments. Here, India has the advantage of offering medicines and drugs at substantially lower costs compared to major Western firms. The time is thus ripe for India to forge a mutually beneficial partnership, taking advantage of the goodwill that exists for it in Africa.[20]

India- East Africa Ties- Historical Experiences

India and East Africa relations can be traced back to ancient times.[21] India and Africa share as civilizations historical links. The Swahili distant trade at the East African Coast reached with its products at Indian ports and Indian traders operated at the Swahili coast. Indian financiers supported the Sultan of Zanzibar. The African slave trade to America and thereby cheaper forms of production lead in essence to the collapse of India's once prominent cotton trade.

Liberated slaves, the so-called *Bombay Africans,* played an important role as Christian missionaries during the early period of British colonialism in Kenya. Indian work-forces and indentured labourers were employed in plantations and railway construction in various African countries in the 19th and early 20th centuries. On the other side one should not forget the little peninsula of Janjira south of Bombay, ruled on Indian soil till 1948 by a small African elite originating from Ethiopia.

With varying degrees of importance, East Africa has been part of India's foreign policy since independence in 1947. Mahatma Gandhi's philosophy, which he successfully put into practice to achieve India's independence, inspired a generation of East African leaders—in their own national liberation campaigns.[22] While Mahatma Gandhi was common icon for Indo- East African relations, it was Jawaharlal Nehru who gave the relationship its political structure.[23] Jawaharlal Nehru, India's prime minister until 1964, referred to Africa as a 'sister continent'.[24] Under him India took definite diplomatic stands on many African issues. Firstly, he supported the decolonisation of African states. Secondly, he took firm stand against racial discrimination in South Africa and broke off India's diplomatic and trade relations from the racist regime. India's engagement with Africa, its diplomacy and interactions in Non-aligned Movement, United Nations, Commonwealth, Afro-Asian organisations were mainly on the lines of anti-colonialism and anti racialism. He was one of the founding fathers of the 1955 Bandung Conference, which in turn paved the way first for the Non-Aligned Movement and later for the Group of 77. In the late 60s, India as a beacon of decolonisation in Africa, as one of the founders of Non-aligned Movement and a leader of Afro-Asian resurgence had been let down during Indo-Chinese War. In the early 70s South-South cooperation was high on the agenda with focus on economic cooperation and both India and East African countries played important roles. The oil crisis of the 70s, however, split the South and South-South cooperation came to exist in name but not in substance. By the end of the 20th century, the relations between India and East African countries witnessed a new turn, with many drivers and rallying points of the 20th century such as de-colonization and racial discrimination disappearing. Moreover, other drivers like Afro- Asian resurgence, the Non-Aligned Movement (NAM) and Collective Self-Reliance of South were subsumed by new forces, resulting in the emergence of a new architecture. With India's liberalisation beginning in 1990s, focus has been more on attracting investment, expanding trade and upgrading infrastructure to fuel growth and development.

Current Forms of Bilateral Engagement

In the recent times India-East Africa cooperation has expanded rapidly. The recent engagements of India with East Africa have been fuelled by pragmatic concerns, namely expanding economic inter-dependence and meeting resource needs. It can be described as the most solid and most cordial bilateral ties in the current international relations. The long – term friendship between both the regions have gone deeper and have become more intense. Both engagement between India and East African countries and between India and the regional organization, East African Community, have developed into a new level. The two sides maintained frequent exchanges of high- level visits, deepened mutual understanding, rendered core interests and concerns and strengthened the practical cooperation with fruitful results in various fields, which have brought great tangible benefits to both sides. This focus has been primarily on trade, investment, development assistance and capacity-building, diaspora resources and peace and stability.

Political Ties

The present political relations, one between independent, self-respecting regions were formally established only after both sides got independence. However, the contemporary relations based on equal regard and concerns for each other can be traced even before East African countries became independent. Since independence the political relationship was driven largely by shared ideological commitments to anti-colonialism, anti-racism, socialism in various forms as well as genuine desire for South-South Cooperation. India instituted 'Award Diplomacy' wherein it conferred award to various African leaders and that also led to exchange of high level visits between India and East African countries. In fact the award diplomacy, rapidly increasing visits and interactions of government and non-government people provided a newer thrust to economic cooperation. A country - wise discussion will make it evident how the political relations have been the basis of India's close- ties with this region.

With Tanzania, India enjoys very warm cordial relations. Its former President Julius Nyerere was conferred Jawaharlal Nehru Award for International Understanding for 1974, and International Gandhi Peace Prize for 1995. Both countries worked closely together in international fora. In the post-Cold War readjustment of policies, India and Tanzania both initiated economic reform programmes around the same time with external relations aimed at broader international political and economic engagement, cultivation of international business relationships and promotion of foreign investment. In recent years Indo-Tanzanian ties have evolved into a modern and pragmatic relationship with greater and diversified economic engagement.

In case of Kenya, India's active support for the Kenyan freedom struggle laid the foundations of a close relationship. Prominent personalities like Sardar Makhan Singh, M.M. Desai and Pio Gama Pinto are remembered even today for their active role in Kenya's struggle for independent nationhood. The exchange of bilateral visits though have not been so frequent, political leadership of both countries has displayed close relations, rapport and understanding of each other's views on bilateral and multilateral issues.

For Uganda Indian independence inspired early Ugandan activists fighting for decolonisation in Uganda. Bilateral relations have been good since independence except during the Amin years. Nearly 55,000 PIOs and 5000 Indians were expelled by President Amin in the early 70s. After President Museveni came to power in 1986, a fraction of the expelled PIOs (eventually 2000) began to return. The government also took steps to restore the properties seized from them. Since the mid-1990s, more Indians have been coming to work in Uganda. Their number is currently estimated to be around 20,000, of which around 15,000 hold Indian passports, while the remaining hold Ugandan, British, Canadian and other passports. Indians and PIOs play a leading role in the Ugandan economy, especially in manufacturing, trade, agro-processing, banking, sugar, real estate, hotels, tourism and information technology. They employ thousands of Ugandans, and are amongst the biggest taxpayers in the country.

Political relations between India and Rwanda have been cordial and have grown steadily over the years. In 1999, Rwanda officially opened its Mission in New Delhi and posted a Charge d' Affaires. Rwanda appointed its first resident Ambassador in New Delhi in 2001. The country became a full member of the COMESA FTA in 2004 and subsequently, in 2007, it was admitted to the EAC. India's bilateral relations with Rwanda got a fillip with Rwanda becoming member of these African Regional Economic Communities (RECs). Recently various high level visits have boosted engagements in various sectors.

In Burundi, since a semblance of stability was restored in the country and the EAC member countries revoked their sanctions and granted membership of EAC, in May 2007, India's bilateral relationship has fostered. The opening of Burundi's resident mission in New Delhi in 2009 and progressive interactions between political leadership of the two countries gave a fillip to the relationship. Both countries enjoy a cordial and friendly relationship.

The political solidarity which both regions have exhibited in the bilateral level has provided lot of impetus to partnerships in various levels. India – Africa Summit has been very significant in this context, as the summit level partnership has led to intensified engagements in various sectors. It calls for partnership and south-south solidarity and focuses on economic empowerment and sustainable development in Africa. Besides the consultative process and the spirit of friendship, sharing of knowledge and experience is another aspect which makes many East African countries relate to India. India's pluralistic democracy, its Parliamentary institutions and procedures, its manner of conducting free and fair elections, its entrepreneur skills attracts the east African countries. They are important lessons which many African countries receive from India. This sharing of experience on political institutions is important aspect of India's non-intrusive support to the development of democratic institutions in these East African countries. This is likely to grow further and become a part of India's investment in sustainable political systems. Besides sharing of experiences both sides agree that institutions of international governance have become anachronistic and need to be democratised and reformed. Both sides had been broadly working together for UN reforms and want to make the UN more representative and democratic. They stand together in global negotiation on critical issues as in multilateral trade negotiations, climate change, fight against terrorism and in international financial institutions.[25]

Trade and Investment

The trade and investment relations between both the sides have grown stronger in the recent times. A country-wise analysis will show the kind of dynamics of trade relations. The region is emerging as an attractive market for Indian goods and services. Investments by Indian private sector have increased substantially after its economic liberalisation in the 1990s. The East African countries such as Kenya, Tanzania, Uganda, Ethiopia, Rwanda have attracted Indian investments in sectors such as Pharmaceuticals, telecommunications, Agriculture and Energy. The long standing cultural, trade and ethnic links that these countries have with India seem to be the important locational factors attracting Indian investments.[26] A cursory view of trade relations between India and the countries of the region will show the economic form of cooperation.

India-Tanzania

India and Tanzania have a vibrant business and commercial relationship driven by the presence of a large community of Tanzanians of Indian origin. India is a leading trading partner of Tanzania's as well as an important source of essential machinery and pharmaceutical products. Many of the top business establishments of Tanzania are owned by members of the Indian origin. India continues to be the largest source of Tanzania's imports for the last three consecutive years.

Tanzania's Major imports from India include mineral fuels, oils, iron & steel, pharmaceuticals, motor vehicles (including auto parts), articles of iron & steel, electrical machinery/ equipment, machinery/ appliances, plastic products including synthetic polymers, rubber items including tiers etc., cotton fabrics, apparel & clothing and cereals. Major exports to India include vegetables, pulses, cashew nuts, raw cotton, gemstones, cloves and other spices, tanning/dyeing extract, wood and articles thereof. India's economic engagement with Tanzania has also increased to a cumulative of US$ 1.314 billion [1992-2009].

Tanzanian's most important hydrocarbon discovery- natural gas reserves at Songo Songo Island located at a distance of 25 kms from the east coast was made by ONGC in 1974. In 1997 ONGC Videsh Limited was requested by TPDC for assistance in the reevaluation of drilled well MITA -1, part of onshore oil exploration program on the Mandawa Block in eastern Tanzania. (OVL provided the consultancy service free of charge) In 2004 Larsen & Toubro Ltd. constructed a gas processing plant at Songo Songo, a 25 km marine pipeline and a 220 km land pipeline (contract valued at $100 million). The Central Mine Planning and Design Institute Limited, Ranchi carried out detailed pre-feasibility and feasibility studies in respect of Mchuchuma-Katewaka coal reserves in the mid-1990s.

The only Indian company currently active in mineral sector in Tanzania is the National Mineral Development Corporation (NMDC);

it had carried out gold exploration in the region south of Lake Victoria in north-west Tanzania during the period 2000 to 2003 and successfully delineated promising targets in Siga Hill area (Kahama dist) and Bulyang' Ombe area (Nzega dist). NMDC has renewed their exploration licence and is carrying out further gold exploration activities in Tanzania.

India-Kenya trade

The East African coast and the west coast of India have long been linked by merchants. The Indian Diaspora in Kenya has contributed actively to Kenya's progress. Many Kenyans have studied in India. In recent times, there is a growing trade (US$ 2.4 billion in 2011-12) and investment partnership. Indian firms have invested in telecommunications, petrochemicals and chemicals, floriculture, etc. and have executed engineering contracts in the power and other sectors.

An India-Kenya Trade Agreement was signed in 1981, under which both countries accorded Most Favoured Nation status to each other. The India-Kenya Joint Trade Committee (JTC) was set up at Ministerial level in 1983 as a follow-up to the Agreement. The JTC has met six times since, the last in October 2010 in Nairobi. A Joint Business Council was set up in 1985 by the Federation of Indian Chambers of Commerce & Industry and the Kenya National Chamber of Commerce & Industry (KNCCI). The KNCCI signed a Memorandum of Understanding with the Confederation of Indian Industry (CII) in 1996.[27]

Recent business promotion events organized in Kenya include: Kenya Plast 2012 organised by the All India Plastics Manufacturers Association (AIPMA in September 2012 in Nairobi; around 35 Indian companies participated at the Printing and Packaging Exhibition organised by an Indian group in Nairobi in September 2012; India Medical Tourism Destination Event in August 2012; Visit of a business delegation from Gujarat (July 2012), ASSOCHAM, FIEO and EPC for EOUs/EPZs delegation of 50 Indian companies in 5th Africa Export & Import Fair 2012 (June 2012); visit of All India Plastics Manufacturers Association delegation (June 2012); participation of 15 Indian companies through CII in 15th Build Expo Africa (May 2012); participation of 25 Indian companies in Buyers Sellers Meet organized by CHEMEXCIL (March 2012); participation of 24 Indian companies through FIEO at the 15th Kenya International Trade Exhibition in Nairobi in November 2011; participation of Plastics Export Promotion

Council (PLEXCONCIL) with 48 Indian exhibitors at the 4th International Exhibition for Plastics, Rubber and Packaging Industry held in Nairobi in July 2011; participation by 11 Indian companies at the Build Expo Kenya exhibition; Buyers Sellers Meet organized by the Engineering Exports Promotion Council (EEPC) in Nairobi in April 2011; 'India: Medical Tourism Destination 2011' organized by Services Exports Promotion Council (SEPC) in Nairobi in March 2011. Tata Africa Holdings (Kenya) and Mahindra & Mahindra were among the companies that participated at the Kenya Motor Show that was held in Nairobi in 2013.[28]

Bilateral trade has been growing and was US$ 2.4 billion for 2011-12, a four percent annual increase according to Indian trade statistics. India's exports were worth nearly US$ 2.3 billion. The figure for the total trade during first six months of 2012-13 is US$ 1.78 billion. According to Kenyan statistics, India-Kenya trade was US$ 1.8 billion during 2011, US$ 1.4 billion in 2010 and US$ 1.1 billion in 2009. Indian exports to Kenya have reached a figure of US$ 1.6 billion (first nine months of 2012). Main Indian exports to Kenya include pharmaceuticals, steel products, machinery, yarn, vehicles and power transmission equipment. Main Kenyan exports to India include soda ash, vegetables, tea, leather and metal scrap.

Tata Chemicals Ltd. acquired Magadi Soda Company Limited in 2005. Several leading Indian public sector insurance companies participate in KenIndia Assurance Co. Ltd. More recent investments by Indian corporates in businesses in Kenya include Essar Energy (petroleum refining), Bharti Airtel, Reliance Industries Ltd. (petroleum retail); Tata (Africa) (automobiles, IT, pharmaceuticals, etc.). Several Indian firms including KEC, Karuturi Ltd., Kalpataru Power Transmission Ltd., Power Grid Corporation of India Ltd., Kirloskar Brothers Ltd., Mahindra & Mahindra, Thermax, WIPRO, Jain Irrigation System Ltd., Punj Lloyd, VIL Ltd., Emcure, Dr. Reddy, Cipla, Cadila, TVS and Mahindra Satyams, etc., have a business presence in Kenya as do the Bank of India and the Bank of Baroda. HDFC has a Representative Office.

The above discussion suggests how India's economic engagement with the region led by Indian private sectors with the support of Indian government initiatives, has grown and expanded between both the countries.

India-Uganda

The volume of bilateral trade has increased from US$ 678.5 million in 2009-10 to US$ 727.9 million in 2010-11 registering an 8 percent growth. India is now the second largest FDI investor in Uganda in 2011. Major exports are: pharmaceuticals, bicycles and bicycle parts, automobile components, small industry & agro-processing machinery, 2-wheelers, textiles, tyres, sports goods etc. Uganda imports almost 30 percent of its pharmaceuticals from India.

A 35-member agri-business delegation from FICCI visited Uganda from August 18-20 August 2011 and had fruitful discussions with President of Uganda, Minister of Agriculture, and Minister of Information & Communications Technology Minister of Trade. They also held a B2B meetings and Business Seminar, co-organised by Uganda Investment Authority and Uganda National Chamber of Commerce & Industry where more than 100 companies from Uganda participated. A number of Indian investors from this sector visited Uganda subsequently.

PIOs and NRIs are estimated to have invested over US$ 1 billion in Uganda in the last two decades. A Double Taxation Avoidance Agreement was signed in Kampala on 30th April, 2004. The agreement came into force with effect from 27th August, 2004.

In June 2010, the Indian company, Bharti Airtel, completed its takeover of the telecommunication company Zain in Uganda and several other countries in Africa. This has deepened the involvement of Indian private sector companies in Uganda's economy.

India-Burundi

The bilateral trade stood at US$ 24.97 million in 2011-12 registering a growth of 52 percent over trade volume of US$ 16.36 million in 2010-11. Bilateral trade figures are as follows: Although the Balance of Trade is heavily in favour of India, India encourages higher Burundian exports to India. India's exports to Burundi are mainly pharmaceuticals and chemicals, machinery and instruments, plastic and linoleum products, transport equipment and rubber manufactured products. The main items that India imports from Burundi are non-electrical machinery, iron and steel. Efforts are also made to further increase the trade between the two countries.

During the last few years, Indian companies have invested in coffee plantation, manufacture of synthetic water tanks, distilleries, computer hardware, hardware stores and paints. Bajaj and TVS have also appointed local dealers in Burundi for sale of two-wheeler motorcycles and three-wheeler auto-rickshaws. Their products are well received in Burundi. A PIO owned company Contec Global Burundi in Bujumbura prints passports and visa stickers for the Burundian government.

The bilateral trade relations discussed above suggests how economic cooperation has been one of the significant drivers. Another major driver behind the growing intensity of engagement with the region has been the large presence of people of Indian Origin. Many key businesses in the East African countries are owned by persons of Indian origin. These include a wide range of areas covering all sectors for example manufacturing, agriculture and food processing, fisheries, transportation, infrastructure development, banking and finance, hotel and tourism among others As PIOs are well established in trade, industry and other professional fields, they are an important heritage resource, which both sides can harness for strengthening bilateral relations. Besides the PIO factor it's the development initiatives provided by India that seem to have bear fruit for the Indian private sector. This is evident from the growing India's trade with East Africa. This picture is also mirrored by Indian investments in East Africa, which come in all shapes and sizes (and ownership patterns), ranging from small family firms to large multinational enterprises in the manufacturing, construction and telecommunication sectors. The developmental partnership has also witnessed an increase in East African exports to India, and in this regard, the Duty Free Tariff Preference Scheme announced by India for the Least Developed countries appears to have been fruitful.

Security Cooperation

Besides the historical connections and economic interactions, some important developments in Indian—East African relationships have been in the security arena. Non–traditional security challenges in the East African region, such as international terrorism, piracy, and the destruction of shipping in the Indian Ocean, remain new set of dynamics that is rapidly expanding relations between India and East African countries.

As discussed earlier for India the region falls under its strategic maritime frontiers. Both sides consider the Indian Ocean to be geostrategic in terms of projected interests whether they are of a political, military, economic, or cultural nature.[29]. Dependency on the Ocean for trade and energy supplies and growing insecurity in the Indian Ocean have made this region important, for collaborating to maintain it as a zone of peace, has been various drivers that have propelled the relationship.

Development Assistance

India has been responding to East Africa's developmental needs through various initiatives. The development cooperation initiatives taken up by India are claimed to be relevant to East Africa's needs and requirements, although the cooperation has been, and still is, minuscule compared with both China and the big traditional donors.[30] It comprises several different programmes which are married to India's interest. They range from capacity building measures, which include training, skill development and scholarships, to Line of Credits (LOC), grants and humanitarian assistance. Historically, the most important development assistance programme has been the Indian Technical and Economic Co-operation (ITEC), which was initiated in 1964 and is still running. According to the Ministry of External Affairs (MEA), India currently transfers Rs 500 million (US$10.3 million) a year via this programme.[31] The MEA has also increased its slots to a number of African countries. ITEC has a sister programme called the Special Commonwealth Assistance for Africa Programme (SCAAP). Basically, this programme makes use of the same aid modalities as ITEC but, unlike ITEC, only targets African countries in the Commonwealth (19 in all). However, not all African Commonwealth countries are targeted with the same degree of eagerness and offered the same conditions. Rather, SCAAP units are allocated according to the perceived importance of the recipient country for India. Hence, countries like Tanzania, Kenya and Uganda (with large Indian diasporas and/or economic importance) receive a relatively large number of slots, while countries with hardly any Indian diaspora, no natural resources and no economic influence receive only a tiny amount of slots.

India also offers scholarships to overseas students (university courses at various levels, professional courses and courses linked to Indian music, dance and art) via the Indian Council for Cultural Relations (ICCR) scholarship scheme. During the 2009-10 academic years some 15 percent of the slots have gone to African countries. Like the ITEC and the SCAAP, India uses this scheme geo-politically. Hence, countries like Tanzania (300),

Uganda (76) Kenya (171), slots are allocated far more scholarships than, say, Rwanda (40), Burundi (14) or in West Africa countries like Cameroon (31) and Guinea Bissau (30).[32]

Besides these India provides development assistance to East Africa in financial terms, which is still insignificant. However it has been boosted massively over the last few years. It is totally linked to India's own capabilities and its interests in the region. Since it is framed as a partnership between equal partners, which can enhance developmental aspect, it has the potential to create a new platform for South-South dialogue. Since 2003 numerous development schemes with a particular focus on East Africa have been launched.

Among the most important initiatives is the Focus Africa Programme (2002-07) totalling US$550 million, administered by the Export Import Bank of India. Essentially, it seeks to enhance commercial links between India and East African countries by offering export subsidies to Indian companies trading with East African nations and tied lines of credit to East African governments and regional entities. The extension of lines of credit is presented by India as a form of development assistance. Indian government needs to find a comfortable space between the rhetoric of South–South coordination and articulating India's national interests and the extension of lines of credit to sub-Saharan African countries could be a route to finding this. There is an open acceptance that these help to promote Indian exports and improve political relations. India has offered NEPAD a US$200 million credit line and has funded the Pan-African E-Network with US$100 million. Besides the LOCs, India has offered bilateral debt relief (by 2008, India had written off debt totalling US$24 million), UN peace-keeping operations and humanitarian assistance to several East African countries.

As development of infrastructure is a priority for East Africa, India has been contributing to this end through the concessional lines of credit .East Africa places a strong emphasis on augmentation of regional connectivity. The role of the private sector in the operationalisation of some of the lines of credit needs no emphasis. This has acquired prominence through the announcement of Lines of Credit to Africa at the two Forum Summits. Prime Minister had announced US$ 5.4 billion as Line of Credit in the First India Africa Forum Summit and an addition US$ 5 billion in this regard during the Second Africa India Forum Summit in Addis Ababa in 2011

Besides the LOC, which is allocated for undertaking different development projects in Africa, Indian Prime Minister Manmohan Singh has pledged, US$700 million for 80 new institutions and training programmes. Under the rubric of IAFS-I and II, India would be establishing more than 100 capacity building institutions in Africa including East Africa encompassing wide variety of fields. There is also a provision for 22,000 scholarships for African students in various academic courses and training programmes including special scholarships focusing on agriculture sciences and fellowships for science and technology.

What is clear in this development assistance programme is that it is based on South–South framework of cooperation with particular attention being given to interaction between equal partners. It has been consultative, responsive and focused on capacity building, infrastructure and human resource development. The initiatives taken up by India for East Africa's development and growth are laudable but they definitely are not wholly altruistic[33], as they are tied to Indian interest.

Regional Level Engagement: India and East Africa Community (EAC)

At the regional level India is engaged in forming partnership with regional organization. India made good progress in developing cooperation with the regional organizations like EAC and COMESA. The regional cooperation programs include several areas like feasibility studies, consultancies, and joint projects in expansion of railway networks. It also includes food and health security, pilot projects on the establishment of micro, small and medium enterprises and ICT for development. India has strength both in medium and small industries as well as in IT areas. India extended large credit lines to the East Africa Development Bank, the PTA Bank for the EAC and COMESA region to help finance sub-regional projects. Like the bilateral level Indian partnership at the regional levels aimed at strengthening the south-south cooperation.

Regional Integration: Opportunities for India-East Cooperation

There are enormous opportunities and possibilities for further Indo-East African cooperation, at the regional level, in the context of the regional integration process. Regional integration is key to Africa's peace, development, and effective engagement with India. The combination of regional integration and India- East Africa ties hold mutual benefit and win win opportunities for India and East Africa. On the other hand the combination will pose challenges to traditional India–East Africa cooperation which is mostly based on bilateral relations, requiring the participants to adjust to multilateral cooperation model and overcome their respective internal and external unfavorable factors.

While East Africa's regional integration is key to regions peace and development, East African regional integration and India East Africa regional cooperation have common interest which complements and promote each other's interests. India-East Africa cooperation in regional integration is an important step to promote each other's development through large scale investments, trade, and unified voice in the International political Affairs. The regional integration provides opportunities for India east Africa political and economic cooperation. Regional cooperation is conducive to promote East Africa's political stability which is the political foundation for India - East Africa Political cooperation. It is conducive to East African countries speaking with one voice and to India and East African countries adoption a common position as developing countries in international affairs. Regional institutional constructions for a unified trade, investments and regulatory environment could create a more favourable political environment for India East Africa economic cooperation. The more progress is made in East Africa's regional integration, the more East Africa's implementation capacity will be strengthen, including the implementation of India East Africa cooperation policies.

Economic integration in East Africa can provide opportunities and space in the breadth and depth for India East Africa economic and trade cooperation. East Africa's economic growth objectives and a clear development strategy, which clarifies development projects in the fields of energy, transportation, health, communication and agriculture in the region provides many opportunities for India and east Africa to strengthen multilateral cooperation in infrastructure, technology transfer, people to people exchange and capacity building and ultimately regional development.

East Africa's economic integration is bound to accord India a huge and untapped market. The expansion of east Africa's commodity markets will be beneficial to the entry of Indian products into east Africa. The effective operation of free trade zones and common markets within EAC will provide a readymade fruitful cooperation platform for India. Regional

Integration in East Africa combined with India East Africa cooperation will benefit East Africa's people.

East African economic integration is conducive to the promotion of investment and trade facilitation. The common meekest would mean that India will face a time saving and efficient unified legal and regulatory system when transacting.

Through regional integration East Africa will experience peace, economic growth, security and benefit of cultural exchanges. East Africa's history of conflict and political instability, and similar economic and industrious structure is mot conducive to internal trade and regional economic integration. While East African integration has a long way to go, it is an irreversible historical process to the development of East Africa. The Indo-East African cooperation is an important strategic opportunity to spur industrialization, urbanization, modernization and sustainable development in India and East Africa

India – Africa Forum Summit process is the framework and platform for India and East African countries to conduct bilateral and multilateral cooperation. Based on bilateral cooperation within the framework, India and East African countries can nurture and promote the combination of India –East Africa cooperation with regional integration in East Africa, to achieve bilateral cooperation complemented with multilateral cooperation, so that India–East Africa cooperation will be more comprehensive and operate at a higher level, on the larger scale, with higher efficiency, and sustainability.

Challenges Ahead

Balancing initiatives for East Africa's developmental needs with its own self-interest remains an onerous challenge for India. India's interaction is primarily economic, led by private sector. Government-to-government as well as academic and civil society interaction is much less. A private sector led India's economic engagement, generates concerns as to whether the economic relations will be able to distinguish qualitatively from the North-South relations.[34] If it would not do so it could affect its goodwill. India has immense goodwill which it needs to preserve, particularly now when competition for influence and resources has intensified among various powers that are trying to increase their foothold in East Africa. It becomes imperative for India to be relevant to East Africa's priorities, needs and expectations for their development and growth.

The challenge for India is also to ensure that its development aid initiatives are effective on ground. It needs to evaluate whether its strategies and methods so far adopted are really making any gainful difference in the ground and are really unique, which it claims? Various analysts observe that India's development assistance initiatives, as discussed in detail, constitutes a combination of tied project aid and scholarships, mainly targeting African countries rich in resources or rich in Indian diasporas, to a large extent mirrors that of China–though on a much smaller scale. They state that China also uses aid to facilitate other financial flows and the modalities are somewhat similar, i.e., comprising technical assistance, few grants, export credits, debt relief and unilateral zero-tariff access for African products. India needs to ensure what it claims- that its engagement with East Africa focused on aid and capacity building- is effective and qualitatively different from others and that African people's concerns are paid attention while pushing its own economic interests.

As far as economic engagement is concerned so far it is observed that India's trade with East Africa has not progressed smoothly. The Indian industry focuses on handful of relatively more advanced economies. The rest of East Africa is yet to feel the industrial strength of India. This is an area that needs attention.[35] It is time to shift from conventional trade to more creative ways of economic cooperation like shifting some of the manufacturing to the African countries which could cut transport costs and more importantly provide employment to the Africans. Some pharmaceutical companies like Ranbaxy have already started this trend and there is a need for more of these initiatives.

Besides economic interaction, which is important, there is a felt need for greater engagement between India and East Africa on issues of a geo-strategic nature. India has always been keen to cooperate with Africa on issues of global security. Owing to their rising global politico-economic profile, both India and East Africa are justifiably expected to highlight the concerns of the developing world at various international fora. This shared responsibility calls for a greater understanding of each other and synchronization of their views and response to a variety of global issues that may have a direct bearing on the development prospects of the peoples of both regions.

Appraisal

India should be able to harmonize its South–South coordination policy and its economic self-interest in order to have a sustainable long term partnership. Business and governments of India and East African countries need to strike deals that not only generate wealth but help eradicate poverty by investing in Africa's peoples. The strategic partnership between India and East Africa should bring tangible solutions for various issues which are included in the African Programme namely NEPAD (The New Partnership for Africa's Development).Particularly expansion of development of infrastructure facilities which will enhance facilitate intra East African trade and economic development in the continent and facilitate trade, economic co-operation and provide improved market access for East African products. As far as visibility in terms of development deliverables of India in East Africa are concerned still much needs to be done. India needs to expand its presence and pay greater attention to implementation of the projects.

End Notes

1   Trends of Knowledge, East Africa Community, http://trends.rifanmuazin.com/East_African_Community

2   Power and Energy Africa, Kenya-The commercial Powerhouse of East Africa, http

3   Jennifer G Cooke , Rwanda, Assessing Risk and Stability, Centre for Strategic And International Studies, June 2011

4   UNDP, Rwanda, Country Context, http://web.undp.org/evaluation/documents/ADR/ADR_Reports/Rwanda/ch2-ADR_Rwanda.pdf

5   Africa Economic Outlook , Burundi, 2012

6   Burundi Investment Promotion Authority, General Economic Information,Newsletter,2011

7   ibid

8   ibid

9   Munene, Macharia, '*Geopolitics, geostrategy and the challenge of ensuring peace in East Africa*', in *21st* Intercultural Seminar, Nairobi, 2012

10   Osita C. Eze, Principal Interests of EU and India in Sub- Saharan Africa, in Dilip Lahiri, Jorg Schultz (ed) *Engaging with a Resurgent Africa*, Macmillan Publishers, Delhi, 2009

11   Julie Pace, Obama Greeted

12   ibid

13   Global Economic Prospects 2011: Regional Annex, Sub Saharan Africa http://siteresources.worldbank.org/ INTGEP/ Resources/335315-1307471336123/7983902-1307479336019/AFR-Annex. pdf, Accessed on 5 June 2011

14   Bajpaee, C., 'The Indian elephant returns to Africa', Online Asia Times, 25 April 2008, http://www.atimes.com/atimes.

15   D. Sharma and D. Mahajan, 'Energising Ties: The Politics of Oil', *South African Journal of International Affairs*, Vol. 14, No. 2, Winter/Spring 2007, pp. 37–53.

16   Alex Vines, India- Africa engagement: Prospects for the 2011 India- Africa forum, Chatham House December 2010.

17   The Hindu, 'Increase of Piracy Attacks off Somalia coast Worrisome: India', United nations, 7 March 2012

18   Cheru, F, 'The rise of china and India in Africa: What should be Africa's Response?', The Nordic Africa Institute, 2010

19   Paul kagame, 'Why Africa Welcomes the Chinese', Guardian, Nov 2, 2009.

20   Ruchita Beri: India Woos Africa. IDSA, 19. 3. 2008,

21   Alex Vines, India's Africa Engagement: Prospects for the 2011 India Africa Forum, Program paper , AFP, Chatham House, UK,2011/01

22   Anirudha Gupta, 'India and Africa South of the Sahara', in Bimla Prasad, (Ed.) *India's Foreign Policy*, New Delhi, 1979.p 269

23   Ajay Dubey, India- Africa Relations: Historical Connections and recent Trends, in Ajay Dubey (ed) Trends in Indo- Africa Relations, Manas Publications, New Delhi.2010

24   A. Sharma, 'India and Africa: Partnership in the 21st Century', *South African Journal of International Affairs*, Vol. 14, No. 2, 2007 p. 20

25   High Commission of India, Nairobi, India-Kenya Relations, http://www. hcinairobi.co.ke/Pages/Kenya_india_ overview.html

26 Aparajita

27 High Commission of India, Nairobi, India-Kenya Relations

28 MEA, GOI, India- Kenya Relations, http://mea.gov.in/Portal/ForeignRelation/ KenyaWebsiteBrief_Dec_2012-font.pdf

29 Macharia Munene, Convergence of Security Interests Kenya and India, in Makumi Mwagiru and Aparajita Biswas (ed) ,India and East Africa Security Relations ,IDIS and PRIASA, April 2012

30 Peter Kragelund, India's Africa Engagement, ARI, 10/2010, 19January 2010.

31 ibid

32 ibid

33 Sudha Ramchandran, India Deepens Africa Role, Asia Times Online, 2 June 2011, http://www.atimes.com/ atimes/South_Asia/MF02Df01.html, accessed on 3 June 2011

34 Ajay Dubey, India- Africa Relations: Historical Connections and recent Trends, in Ajay Dubey (ed)Trends in Indo- Africa Relations, Manas Publications, New Delhi.2010

35 Lalit Mansingh, 'Engaging a Resurgent Africa: India's Choices' in Dilip Lahiri, Jorg Schultz (ed) *Engaging with a Resurgent Africa*, Macmillan Publishers, Delhi, 2009

Chapter - 2

India and East Africa: Development Cooperation

The commerce between India and Africa will be of ideas and services, not of manufactured goods against raw materials after the fashion of the western exploiters.

(Mahatma Gandhi, in Bhattacharya 2010, p. 63)

The development partnership discourse and practices in Africa, since long has been dominated by Western advanced states. However, with emerging powers such as India, China and Brazil, scaling up their development programmes, the landscape of development cooperation in Africa is changing. The model of development partnership adopted by the emerging powers is based on the framework of South-South cooperation (SSC), which is much a wider concept than that of "aid" as defined by the Development Assistance Committee (DAC) of Organisation for Economic Cooperation and Development (OECD). In terms of approach, principles, modalities and outcomes, the emerging powers are different from the DAC members. But among themselves they are also distinct from each other with regard to their development policies they pursue in Africa. The African countries have welcomed the development assistance provided by emerging powers, as it not only provides opportunities to them, but also political leverage. India on its part has been proactively contributing to Africa's development since long. But in recent years it has been in limelight for its enhanced involvement in development partnership programmes.

This chapter will focus on India's development cooperation in East Africa. It aims to understand how India, an emerging power, is partnering with East Africa in their development process. It argues that India's development partnership in East Africa is linked to its strengths and foreign policy objectives and is different from the traditional donors as well as other emerging powers. From a recipients' perspective it provides comparative advantage. However, there is a need to constantly evaluate and assess its effectiveness in terms of delivering development in East Africa.

In East Africa the Indian government has launched a number of initiatives to strengthen cooperation between both the regions. India is pursuing a development cooperation model of trade, training and technology based on the south-south cooperation model, in respect of East Africa. This is infused with a development-centric approach that is aimed at enhancing trade, transferring technology, capacity building and human resource development.

There are two instruments through which India extends development assistance: the LOC extended by the Export-Import (Exim) Bank of India and the traditional technical assistance predominately managed by the country's ministry of external affairs. Overall, Indian development assistance has grown.

Needless to say, it is difficult to ascertain precisely the volume and types of India's development assistance to East Africa because complete and disaggregated data is hard to find. The available data does not make a distinction between what the OECD's (Organisation for Economic Cooperation and Development) development action committee would define as aid and what is export credit, a problem that also holds true to Chinese aid to Africa.

As will be made clear later in this chapter, a large part of what India spends is on development assistance in human resource development and capacity building. India is increasingly aware of the need to improve the material standards of East African people in order that the region's economic leverage is increased. India has wealth of experiences in various sectors which it believes in sharing with the East African countries for their growth and development.

Historical Evolution of India's development Partnership with East Africa

India has been a provider of development assistance to East African countries since its independence, but its role and contribution has gained momentum more recently as a result of its growing economic and political influence in the global community. In contrast to the traditional donors OECD/DAC countries until today India do not have any publicly declared policy paper or standards of development cooperation.[1]

The guiding principles for its foreign policy and its development cooperation are founded in the Panchsheel/Bandung Principles. From the time of its emergence as an independent state, Prime Minister Jawaharlal Nehru laid the foundation for India's South- South Cooperation Policy (SSC) in 1947. He said India saw linkages with other developing countries as an important policy priority. Self reliance and self–help was the key component of this policy and characterized by three fundamental principles mutual respect, equality and win-win situation.

A series of initiatives in line with the mutually supportive approach of South-South Cooperation (SSC) were undertaken well before the 1955 Bandung conference. In 1949 the Indian Government established seventy scholarships (increased to 100 in 1952) with the aim of promoting cultural relations with African countries in general and East African countries in particular.

From the beginning of the 1960s, as a direct consequence of the competition with China, India began to target countries in Africa[2] through its ITEC programme, which included East African countries such as Ethiopia, Kenya, Sudan, Tanzania and Uganda. India however lost its interest in development aid as a foreign policy tool in the 1980s and 1990s and changed its perception of aid later in this millennium, now seeing it as an instrument to gain political and economic influence. This shift, on the part of India, from mostly being an aid recipient to also being an aid donor, was perceived as a means to get more international political leverage and ultimately obtain a seat in (an enlarged) UN Security Council. This change in India's external development policy was at the initiative of the Ministry of Finance. In this regard 2003 was a landmark. The budget speech of 2003, sparked the new importance given to development cooperation, which set the unsuccessful 'India Development Initiative' in motion.[3]

The mandate of this initiative was to foster techno-economic cooperation and intellectual cooperation and promote India's interest in overseas market. Under this initiative numerous schemes were launched in East African countries. Hardly any of these would be categorized as aid in a strict DAC (Development Assistance Committee) sense of the term. Rather, they were amalgamations of grants, technical assistance, Line of Credits preferential bilateral loans and project partnerships.[4] India even offered UN peace-keeping operations, and humanitarian assistance to several African countries including East African.

The April 2008 India-Africa Summit in New Delhi, as stated earlier marked the culmination of India's renewed focus on East African countries as a part of broader development cooperation engagement with the countries of Africa. This was spurred by the realisation that political ties have lagged behind the growing economic ties between India and African countries including East African countries. It produced a Framework of cooperation that later translated into Action Plan that committed itself to the establishment of various cooperative mechanisms which were relevant to the needs of East African countries. Among the many initiatives that India announced at the summit which benefited East African countries are:

- An increase of the existing level of credit to Africa from about $2 billion to $5.4 billion by 2013.

- A duty-free tariff preference scheme for 34 least developed African countries. The scheme will cover 94 per cent of total tariff lines and products, such as cotton, cocoa, aluminium ores, copper ores, cashew nuts, cane sugar, clothing and nonindustrial diamonds.

- The doubling of trade from $25 billion to $50 billion by 2011.

- A $500 million budget allocation for capacity building and human resource development, expanding existing training programmes for African students and technocrats.

Support to Africa's regional integration efforts and provision of financial support to the AU and the New Partnership for Africa's Development (NEPAD). This includes a $200 million line of credit to NEPAD. [5]

Through these various developments partnership programmes India is presently steadily consolidating its expanding and much closer ties with East Africa. The table below shows India's development cooperation programmes broadly.

Table1: India's Development Cooperation Programmes in Africa/East Africa (1950-2008)

Period	1950	1964 →		2002-2007		2004 →
Form	Scholarships	Tied grants & technical assistance		Tied Credit lines and TA	Credit lines	Tied credit lines
Aim	Strengthen cultural relations	Enhance trade and investment relations	Enhance trade relations with Africa	Promote trade and investments		

Table 2. Continued

Responsible entity	Indian Council for Cultural Relations	Economics Affairs Department, Ministry of External Affairs 21		Export-Import Bank of India		Ministry of Commerce and Industry
Country focus	Mostly neighbouring countries. Africa (15 percent)	Mostly neighbouring countries	19 African Commonwealth countries	All 22	> 50 percent African countries. Specific focus on oil-rich nations	8 West African countries
Sectoral focus	Education	ICT (50 percent), rural development, health		ICT, infrastructure, and agriculture		
Modality	Stipends	Training (40 percent), project aid, TA, study trips and humanitarian assistance23		Projects & TA		

Sources: (Agrawal, 2007; Chanana, 2009; ICCR, 2009; Katti, Chahoud, & Kaushik, 2009; MEA, 2009a; Naidu, 2008; Naidu & Herman, 2009).

Current shifts and trends

- Continued and growing focus on training and technical assistance

- Growing focus on ICTs

  » Pan Africa e-network

- Growing focus on Lines of Credit: heavily tied

- Significant contribution to UN peace-keeping, World Food Programme

- Changes in the institutional structures of development cooperation

  » Increased role for Ministry of Commerce and the EXIM Bank

  » Discussions over an 'India International Development Cooperation Agency

- Closer ties to the private sector

Current Operating LOCs between India and East African countries

- Republic of Tanzania – Agricultural Mechanization (tractor, pump and equipment/40 million USD)

- Federal Democratic Republic of Ethiopia – Sugar processing industry (640 million USD) and energy transmission and distribution project (65 million USD)

- Eastern African Development Bank - For financing export of eligible goods and services to Uganda, Kenya and Tanzania (5 million USD)

- African Exim Bank - To facilitate purchase of capital and engineering goods, industrial manufactures, consumer durables and services and other items in any of the Afreximbank's Member States (30 million USD)

EXIM Bank operative Lines of Credit as of October 2011 (total value $ 7054 million

Eastern and Southern African Trade and Development Bank (PTA Bank) - For financing export of eligible goods and services to any PTA bank member countries viz., Burundi, Comoros, Djibouti, Egypt, Eritrea, Ethiopia, Kenya, Malawi, Mauritius, Rwanda, Seychelles, Somalia, Sudan, Tanzania, Uganda, Zambia and Zimbabwe (40 million USD)

1. Africa   54 percent

2. Asia   43 percent

3. Latin America, Caribbean   1 percent

4. Oceania   1 percent

5. CIS countries   1 percent

Regional distribution of LOC Total value USD 3781 MN

- East Africa   35 percent

- West   35 percent

- Central   10 percent

- North   15 percent

- South   5 percent

Institutional Mechanisms and Nature of Development Assistance to East Africa

Primarily there are two instruments through which India extends development assistance: the Line of Credit (LOC) extended by the Export-Import (EXIM) Bank of India and the traditional technical assistance predominately managed by the country's Ministry of External Affairs (MEA). It is difficult to account precisely the exact value and quantum of India's development assistance to Africa because complete and disaggregated data is hard to find [6]. India's development cooperation with East African countries is done at bilateral as well as multilateral level. It is implemented by various ministries and institutions with the Ministry of External Affairs (MEA) as the leading ministry. The MEA extends bilateral and technical assistance through its various missions. The Department of Economic Affairs of the Ministry of Finance (MoF) is normally approached by MEA with country specific disbursements.[7] The bilateral aid that India provides is mainly in the form of training and capacity building endeavours, technical assistance, project assistance and provisions for humanitarian assistance like medical products. In recent years funding related to infrastructural construction and maintenance has also experienced major increases.

The bulk of Indian bilateral development assistance to East African countries is devoted to training, capacity building, project-related consultancy services, deputation of experts, study tours and other 'soft' investments, although the country also supports a number of capital projects financed by export credit extended through the EXIM Bank.[8]At the forefront of our partnership with Africa are the areas of human resource development and capacity building.[9] India is supporting institutional capacity building at the pan-African, regional and bilateral levels. It is setting up scores of institutions in areas as diverse as food processing, agriculture, textiles, weather forecasting and rural development. A pan-African e-network linking schools and hospitals across East Africa with top institutions in India has the potential to make Indian expertise in healthcare and education accessible to the East African people. Among the most important technical assistance programmes for capacity building are the Indian Technical and Economic Cooperation (ITEC) Programme and the Special Commonwealth African Assistance Programme for Africa (SCAAP).

ITEC Programme

According to the Ministry of External Affairs, India currently transfers Rs 500 million (USD 10.3 million) a year via this programme, which includes sizeable contribution to East African countries. The Africa-India Forum Summit (2008) agreed to enhance programmes of training and capacity building for health professionals. Basically, ITEC uses a slots system to allocate aid. Slots may then be exchanged into five different aid modalities, namely: training of personnel in India, project aid, technical assistance, study trips and humanitarian assistance. These modalities comprise a variety of different sectors including numerous courses to enhance production and trade competitiveness in African small and medium sized companies as well as courses focusing on intellectual property rights and infrastructure project preparation. These modalities are allocated according to the perceived importance of the recipient country for India (just like the ITEC slots). Hence, countries like Kenya, Tanzania Uganda, with large Indian diasporas and/or economic importance) receive a relatively large number of slots. The ITEC slots are adjusted on a yearly basis and recently some of them have got their ITEC slots increased. These slots have become important avenues of capacity building (MEA, 2009a, 2009b).

For instance the slots given to Ethiopia has been very useful in the form of deputation of experts, human resource development for capacity building, supply of equipment in the fields of industry, agriculture, transport, health, irrigation and water resources. In 2007-08, the number of training slots offered by India was 25. In 2009-10, it was increased to 90 slots and they were fully utilized. For the year 2010- 2011, it was enhanced to 120 slots which have also been fully utilized.

Similarly for the year 2012-2013, two hundred slots have been allotted for Tanzania. About 47 reputed institutes spread all over India, impart training in roughly 150 disciplines in various fields including finance, banking, information technology, telecommunication, English courses, management, small and medium enterprises, rural development.

India also offers scholarships to overseas students (university courses at various levels, professional courses and courses linked to Indian music, dance and art) via the Indian Council for Cultural Relations (ICCR) scholarship scheme. Like the ITEC and the SCAAP, India uses this scheme geo-politically. Hence, countries like Kenya, Uganda, and Tanzania, Ethiopia in East Africa are allocated far more scholarships than, say, Cameroon, Guinea, and Togo.

Like the ITEC the Special Commonwealth Assistance for Africa Programme (SCAAP) programme uses the same aid modalities. The modalities are also allocated according to the perceived importance of the recipient country for India (just like the ITEC slots). Countries such as Kenya, Tanzania, and Uganda (large Indian diasporas and/ or economic importance) receive a relatively large number of slots, while countries with hardly any Indian diasporas, no natural resources and no economic influence receive only a tiny amount of slots.

In addition, the ITEC programme provides scholarships to African students who take regular academic courses in India[10], via the Indian Council for Cultural Relations (ICCR) scholarship scheme. Countries like Ethiopia, Kenya, Tanzania, and Uganda have been allocated far more scholarships as compared to many African countries.

Another novel far-reaching initiative by India has been the launch of the Pan-African e-Network in February 2009. The project would go a long way in bridging the digital divide and give major benefits to East African countries in capacity building through skill and knowledge development of students, medical specialists and for medical consultation thereby accelerating development on the African continent. It ensures connectivity for telemedicine, tele -education, internet video conferencing and also supporting e-Governance, e-Commerce, infotainment, resource mapping, meteorological services etc. This is a major salient contribution in the IT sector in expanding educational facilities and cheaper healthcare. It is helping in augmenting capacity building of human resource by way of imparting quality education to students, through the best Indian Universities/ Educational Institutions and providing tele-medicine services by way of on-line medical consultations to the medical practitioners in the patient-end locations from Indian medical specialists in various disciplines/ specialties/ sub-specialties". In this way India is making a major contribution in human capital formation, infrastructure development all of which are essential for sustainable development.

After the April 2008 India- Africa Summit India has tried to expand its development cooperation linkages in various parts of East Africa. India has tried to consolidate the flow of funds through effective partnerships. The strength of these partnerships has been its non-prescriptive nature.[11] India does not instruct, impose or even demand certain approaches or projects in Africa, but offer to contribute to the achievement of development aspirations of the East African countries. India is committed to the establishment of new cooperative bodies under this partnership framework of agreement.

India is in the process of establishing the India- Africa Institute of Foreign Trade in Kampala, Uganda, while Burundi would host the Institute of Education Planning and Administration, which would train professional to plan and manage higher education across East Africa. Such endeavours to invest in human resource development are the vital aspect of India's partnership model of engagement.

India's private sector, though not government led or government subsidized yet are making serious contribution to the development of East Africa, fully governed by the logic of commercial opportunities. The combined net flows from India to East Africa emerging from government credits and private sector investments form another part of sustainable developmental cooperation, which has in turn given Indian companies to seek opportunities in East Africa.

Pharmaceutical Company in Kenya and Tanzania is a good example. Indian pharmaceutical companies like Ranbaxy and Cipla are not just supplying low cost generic drugs, they have set up production facilities there. Another example is Indian investment in agriculture and horticulture, which contributes mainly to exports, with Indian firms increasingly getting attracted by the large tracts of fertile land available in many East African countries like Ethiopia, Tanzania, Kenya and Mozambique.

Although this has garnered lot of criticism about "land grabbing", it has been made clear by the government of Ethiopia and many other East African countries that Indian companies are welcome there. Ethiopia in particular has 3 million hectares of land that it wants to lease to foreign agricultural companies. According to Meles Zenawi they wanted to develop their lands to feed themselves rather than admire the beauty of fallow fields while people starve.[12]

Food security

Another uniqueness that India enjoys is that farmers from North India (Punjab) have gone to East African countries to train farmers about innovative farming techniques. Some East African countries have invited Indian farmers and provided agricultural land on long term lease while some farmers are going to East African countries because of cheaper land and vision of profitability.

The Indian government is supporting soft loans in agriculture sector to several East African nations and deputing agricultural experts to assist in solving food security and value addition. It is reported that "In June 2011 the Indian Council of Agriculture Research (ICAR) teams visited Ethiopia, Kenya and other countries of the African continent to understand problems there and cooperate for assisting Africa increase agricultural production"[13]. The ICAR is also keen that students from East African countries come to India to study agriculture and related subjects and have introduced scholarships and fellowships to attract them while several students from neighbouring countries come regularly for higher studies.

Many Indian food companies are keen to set up food processing units. It will help to tap the domestic East African market and generate revenues but also contribute towards the food security in the region.

The Government of India too is playing the role of a catalyst in helping its food and agriculture companies increase their presence in East Africa. India is encouraging to place Foreign Direct Investments (FDI) in East Africa which will not only allow fund infusion but access to improved technology from India to East Africa. Such initiatives will help East Africa have access to improvised technology transfer from India and the latter will need to adopt or improvise the same without investing in new ones.

When Indian food and agri majors participate in joint venture pacts with African companies it leads to faster and easier technology adoption and assimilation. Further, there is scope for Indian companies to build forward linkages like contract farming helping the agri sector in Africa to integrate agri supply chain with processing plant or retailing business, according to an industry observer. Officials from the Institute of Social and Economic Change, Bengaluru, opine that fertile land access in Africa will support feeding many hungry mouths, if agricultural experts from countries in Asia including India provide the required support to grow and sustain sowing and harvesting activities.

Indian companies in the African countries view only gains as it firstly helps to infuse the right technology and secondly generate local employment. There is a significant presence of Indian agricultural firms and food processing companies in Africa. These include Tata Group, Karuturi Global, Shapoorji Pallonji & Co, BHO Bio, Jaipurias of RJ Corp, Whitefield Cotton Farm, Verdanata Harvests, S&P Energy Solutions, Sannati Agro Farm Enterprises and Ruchi Soya.

Food clusters

At the Second India-Africa Summit in 2011 at Addis Ababa, packages given by Government of India to Africa cover development of food clusters only for exports in Africa. Field Fresh Foods Pvt. Ltd is a joint venture between Bharti Enterprises and Del Monte Pacific Ltd. The company offers branded Field Fresh fruits & vegetables across Indian and international markets and Del Monte branded processed foods & beverages will also be exported to Africa, according to Sanjay Nandrajog, CEO, Field Fresh Foods.

Petonia Food, a leading frozen vegetarian food range marketed under the brand name Mother's Kitchenette, is currently engaged in exports of frozen foods to the Middle-East, Dubai, Australia and Africa. "The latter is an important destination," stated Mihir Parekh, CEO/MD, Petonia Foods, in an earlier interaction with F&B News.

Karuturi Global Ltd has over three lakh hectares to grow cereal, pulses and palm. Ruchi Soya has 25,000 hectares to grow soya beans; Sannati Agro Farm Enterprises has 10,000 hectares to cultivate pulses, rice and cereals. There are also spice and tea majors looking at Africa with considerable interest.

Leased land concept

According to the Confederation of Indian Industry (CII), the tax concessions and leased land concept have seen companies here opt for an African trail even if they are remotely associated with agriculture and food processing. For instance, infrastructure major Shapoorji Pallonji & Co received 50,000 leased hectares in Ethiopia and is likely to consider its foray into agriculture in the coming years. There is also considerable interest evinced for the tea gardens in Africa which are known to have some of the best black teas in the world. The regions of Malawi, Kenya and Tanzania are home to the best tea estates, according to a food exporter.

An official pointed out that there were over 70 Indian companies, which were now working to enter Africa to start farming activities, as there was huge scope for growth in Ethiopia, Malawi, Kenya, Uganda, and Rwanda.

According to industry information garnered from various sources: The Tata Group too has land leased in Uganda to run a pilot agricultural project. Another leading industry, Jaipurias of RJ Corp leased 50-acre model dairy farm to expand its presence from the Uganda and Kenya and tap other countries of Africa to market its range of milk by-products.

There are also efforts to acquire tea estates by Indian companies. High price of tea garden acquisition in India is driving many companies to Africa. The B M Khaitan-owned McLeod Russel India, said to be the largest integrated tea company in the world, acquired Uganda's Rwenzori Tea Investments. Borelli Tea Holdings of the UK, a wholly-owned subsidiary of McLeod Russel India and Rwenzori Tea Investments has six estates to produce 15 million kg of tea annually. B K Birla's Jay Shree Tea & Industries, bought three tea gardens in East Africa at Rwanda and Uganda. Further, Dhunseri Tea & Industries is scouting for acquisitions in East Africa.

In addition India is strengthening its ties with East Africa through lines of credit, foreign direct investment (FDIs), and technical assistance.

Development Assistance to East African Countries

Kenya

India offers development assistance to Kenya in the form of loans and credit. This includes a loan of Rs. 50 million to Government of Kenya in 1982 and Lines of Credit by EXIM Bank to Industrial Development Bank Capital Ltd.

An Agreement on extension of a Line of Credit of US$ 61.6 million by EXIM Bank of India to the Government of Kenya for utilization in the power transmission sector was signed during the visit of Prime Minister Raila Odinga to India in November 2010.

In 1998, an MoU was signed between the National Small Industries Corporation and Kenya Industrial Estates Ltd. In 2003, an MoU was signed between India Trade Promotion Organisation and Export Promotion Council of Kenya.

Kenya is among countries planned to be covered by the Pan African e-Network Project that was launched in 2007. An Agreement was signed in July 2009 between TCIL and the Kenyan Ministry of Information and Communication regarding the project. Equipment was delivered by TCIL in 2010. VSAT terminals have been installed at Kenyatta National Hospital in Nairobi (August 2011) and at Maseno University Varsity Plaza for Learning Centre in Kisumu (September 2011).

The High Commissioner led the Indian delegation at the Summit on the Horn of Africa Crisis hosted by Government of Kenya in Nairobi on September 8-9, 2011. On September 14, 2011 the Government of India announced that it will provide humanitarian assistance of US$ 8 million to the countries affected by famine and drought in the Horn of Africa i.e. Somalia, Kenya and Djibouti. The assistance was being provided through the World Food Programme.

Tanzania

India gifted 5,000 tons each of wheat and rice to Tanzania faced with food scarcity arising from drought conditions (aid promised in April 2003, arrived in May 2004). In September 2002 India gifted two raw cashew nut processing plants in Tanzania. Small Industry Development Organisation (SIDO) of Tanzania was established by National Small Industries Corporation Ltd [NSIC] of India in November 2007.

Two Indian funded projects were set up: A Centre of Excellence in ICT by C-DAC; and the Pan African e-Network Project by TCIL. The Centre is named "*India-Tanzania Centre for Excellence in Information and Communication Technology*" [ITCoEICT]. The ITCoEICT was set up at Dar-es-Salaam Institute of Technology with one Param High Speed Super Computer and 10 remote regional centres. The Pan African e-Network Project entails both Tele-education Centre in the University of Dar-es-Salaam and Telemedicine Centre in the Ocean Road Cancer Institute and a VVIP hotline and audio visual conferencing facility set up in State House under this project.

Government of India has extended a Line of Credit of US$ 40 million for financing Tanzanian agriculture sector. The LOC was signed on 5 June 2009. The Tanzanian Prime Minister, Mr. Mizengo Pinda inaugurated the first consignment of 288 tractors on 07th October 2010 which have arrived in Tanzania, of the total of 1860 tractors.

The 2nd Line of Credit of US$ 36.56 million for supply of Indian vehicles to the Government of Tanzania was approved and Mr. Mustafa H. Mkulo, Minister for Finance and Economic Affairs of the Government of the United Republic of Tanzania visited India to sign the Agreement on 28th March, 2011 for the GOI-supported Exim Bank Line of Credit of US$ 36.56 million on the sidelines of the 7th CII Exim Bank Conclave on India Africa Project Partnership in New Delhi from 27-29 March, 2011.

The third Line of Credit of US$ 180 million was announced by Prime Minister during his State visit to Tanzania from 26-28 May, 2011 for development of water supply projects in Dar-es-Salaam and coastal regions.

Prime Minister also announced a grant of US$ 10 million for projects in social and educational sectors, projects for which is to be identified by the Tanzanian side during his State visit to Tanzania from 26-28 May, 2011.

Prime Minister announced Vocational Training Centre and a grant of US$ 100,000/- for Zanzibar for purchase of laboratory equipment for schools during his State visit to Tanzania from 26-28 May, 2011.

The fourth Line of Credit of US$ 35 million for a bio-diesel project was approved by the Government of India in November, 2011.

Tanzania is one of the largest beneficiaries of the ITEC/SCAAP programme. The two countries signed in 1966 an Agreement on Friendship and Technical, Economic and Scientific Cooperation, within the framework of which ITEC cooperation has been extended to Tanzania since 1972. Starting with 24 trainees annually, the number has gradually increased to the current 175 in 2010, and the total number of trainees till date has exceeded 1200. For 2011-12, 200 slots were been sanctioned.

Tanzania is a major beneficiary of Indian scholarships and other educational assistance, including self-financing seats in India's institutes of higher learning. Almost all official agencies in Tanzania have Indian trained alumni. 18 scholarships offered annually (in 2011) by ICCR under the Commonwealth Scholarship/Fellowship Plan and General Cultural Scholarship Scheme. About five thousand Tanzanian students are estimated to be in India on a self-financed basis.

Cooperation in Human Resources

Cooperation in the sector constituted an important aspect of bilateral relations. It emanates from Tanzania's request. On the Indian side EDCIL coordinated the cooperation. 28 Indian professors/lecturers have been deputed to the University of Dodoma. A Delegation from EDCIL, led by CMD, visited Tanzania from 7-17 April 2010.

There are four lecturers from India working in two private universities (Zanzibar University and College of Education) in Zanzibar, and two more Indian lecturers are likely to join the University of Zanzibar. However, Zanzibar Ministry of Education still needs lecturers and teachers for SUZA and local schools.

A Bangalore-based Vigyan Educational Foundation set up in Dar es Salaam in 1996, an International Medical and Technological University, the first private university in Tanzania. A proposal for setting up of super specialty hospital in Tanzanian is being actively pursued between Apollo Hospitals, India and National Social Security Fund (NSSF) of Tanzania.

Uganda

To assist Uganda in its infrastructure and human resource development, India has offered setting up of three institutions namely, India-Africa Institute of Foreign Trade, Food Processing Business Incubation Centre and Material Testing Laboratory.

Following the First India-Africa Forum Summit, Uganda was nominated by the African Union to host the India-Africa Institute of Foreign Trade (IAIFT). Following the stake-holders workshop held at Kampala in June, 2011 by Indian Institute of Foreign Trade (IIFT) and Ministry of Trade, Industry and Cooperatives of Uganda, the officials of Ugandan Ministry of Trade and Ugandan Management Institute (UMI) visited India and finalized the MoUs to be signed between (i) IIFT and Government of Uganda; and (ii) between IIFT and UMI. After signing of the MoUs, the institute was expected to become functional during the first half of 2012.

Following the Second India-Africa Forum Summit in Addis Ababa in May, 2011, Government of India proposed setting up of a Food Processing Business Incubation Centre in Uganda. The proposal was welcomed by the Ugandan side. The centre would provide support to the local entrepreneurs to enhance their skills in food processing and to acquaint themselves with the latest technologies and equipment used in this industry and would also create additional jobs for the rural youth. A delegation of Indian experts is expected to visit Uganda soon to discuss the modalities for setting up the Centre.

In addition to the above, Inter-Governmental Authority on Development (IGAD) and Economic Community of Central African States (ECCAS) have selected Uganda as one of the countries for setting up of Material Testing Laboratories through RECs. The laboratory would provide for material testing facilities to test soil, aggregates, bitumen and cement concrete material for the road sector. The laboratory would be made operational in about 12-18 months after signing of the requisite agreements. Indian Academy of Highway Engineers (IAHE), which is the implementing agency on behalf of GoI, will run, maintain, supervise and manage the laboratory for three years after commissioning and will also organize training and training of trainers programme.

Following the visit of Ugandan Minister of Energy and Mineral Development, Hon. Ms. Irene Muloni to India in December 2011, the two governments have agreed to enhance cooperation in the hydrocarbon sector.

Following the visit of a three-member delegation from Ministry of Textiles to Uganda in September 2011, India and Uganda are discussing the scope of engagements in terms of R&D and technology support, investment facilitation, supply of seed and market linkage.

Under the Pan-African E-Network Project, a Tele-medical centre has been set up in Mulago Hospital where several diagnostic equipment, such as ECG, X-Ray, Ultra Sound, etc., have also been set up as part of the project. The centre is connected to 11 reputed Indian hospitals for medical consultations and also for continuing medical education. The project was formally inaugurated by H.E. Mr. S.M. Krishna, External Affairs Minister from the Indian side and H.E. Mr. Sam Kutesa, Foreign Minister on the Ugandan side at Makerere University Tele-Education Centre in August, 2010.

Training. An estimated 1000 Ugandan students are presently studying in Indian universities. Over the years, thousands of Ugandans have studied in Indian colleges and universities, especially in Pune, Bangalore and Delhi. They include children of many high-ranking Ugandan ministers and officials. There is an APTECH franchise in Kampala and a branch of Sikkim-Manipal University. ITEC deputationists have taught at the University of Mbarara.

Under the ITEC/SCAAP programme, 61 slots were allocated to Uganda for the year 2011-12. Following the announcement made by Hon'ble Prime Minister of India during the 2nd India-Africa Forum Summit held in Addis Ababa in May 2011, an additional 15 slots were allocated to Uganda during the year 2011-12, taking the total to 76 slots. Seeing Uganda's growing interest in ITEC/SCAAP Programme, during a midterm review of the utilization of slots, Government of India has increased the allocation of slots to Uganda to 85 for the current year.

Uganda has also availed of the services of ITEC experts. Twenty three scholarships are offered to Uganda annually from 2008-09 by ICCR, under three schemes, for courses of study in Indian universities.

Uganda has been allocated one slot for 52nd NDC course at the prestigious National Defence College. Ugandan defence personnel have also been attending various training courses in Indian defence institutes under ITEC-II.

Uganda is also actively participating in the training programmes offered as part of the implementation of decisions of India-Africa Forum Summit.

An Indian Army Training Team (IATT) led by a Brigadier and consisting of two Colonels and one Group Captain is in Uganda since February, 2010 at the Ugandan Army's Senior Command and Staff College, Kimaka for a period of three years, under the ITEC programme.

A delegation from National Defence College (NDC) led by Brig. A.K. Jha visited Uganda from 15-20 May 2011. It was first ever visit to Uganda by an NDC team. The team had an opportunity to interact with various leaders and high ranking officials of the Ugandan Government.

Rwanda

India's engagement with Rwanda is at three levels viz. at the African Union (AU) level, at level of the Regional Economic Communities (RECs) and at the bilateral level.

Moreover, India's engagement with Rwanda has been consultative, response-based and focused on developing Rwandan capacities and human capital. Indian assistance to Rwanda has been guided mainly by the announcements made by India at the India- Africa Forum Summits in 2008 and 2009.

Following the first India Africa Forum Summit (IAFS-I), Rwanda was nominated by the AU as one of the recipients to host the India-Africa Vocational Training Centre (VTC). An agreement between the National Small Industries Corporation Ltd. (NSIC) and Government of Rwanda is likely to be signed soon.

During IAFS-II, India announced establishment of several institutions in Africa. As a part of its initiatives under IAFS-II, India is establishing the India-Africa Entrepreneurship Development Centre (IAEDC) in Rwanda. While recognizing that entrepreneurship is one of the most important factors in the development of a country's economy and an antidote to unemployment, the centre is committed to nurture the spirit of entrepreneurship in the country through education, training and business advisory services. The centre aims to foster business culture among the youth, both educated and not-so-educated, by orienting them to think in terms of entrepreneurship as a viable career option. The modalities of the project are being processed.

At IAFS-II, India also offered, among other things, eight Agricultural Seed Production cum-Demonstration Centre, one each for the 8 RECs. The EAC has decided to locate one centre in Rwanda. The Rwandan Government has accepted the proposal. The centre is a testimony to India's effort to help the region achieve food security.

Another institute is a Food Testing Laboratory (FTL) which India is setting-up in Rwanda as per announcements made under IAFS-II. ICRISAT, the Indian implementing agency and Rwanda Bureau of Standards (RBS) are working towards the establishment of the institute.

India has extended an EXIM Bank Line of Credit worth US$ 80 million to Rwanda for construction of a 27.5 MW hydroelectric power project on the Nyabarongo River. The project is being executed by Bharat Heavy Electric Limited (BHEL) and Angelique International Ltd. The foundation stone was laid in December 2008 and the project is expected to be completed in 2014, with the possibility of commissioning one turbine at an early date. After the completion of the project, Rwanda's electricity generation capacity will be augmented by almost 50 percent.

Following the visit of Hon. Shri Arun Yadav, Minister of State for Agriculture and Food Processing Industries to Rwanda in May 2011, WAPCOS Limited, a Government of India undertaking, has signed an MoU with the Rwandan Ministry of Agriculture and Animal Resources for identification, planning, implementation and management of irrigation projects in Rwanda. The project report was submitted to the Rwandan Government in January, 2012.

Under the Pan Africa e-Network project, tele-medicine and tele-education centres were established in Rwanda in 2009 with an aim to enable Rwandan doctors to consult their Indian counterparts, and ensure world-class medical consultation and treatment for patients and education for students. The initiative will help Rwandan access medical care and education from India at a fraction of cost. The project is operating successfully.

Trilateral Cooperation

In June 2012, Rwanda accepted the Indo-US-Rwanda Trilateral Open Government Platform Initiative developed under the India-US Dialogue on Open Government which enables the participating nation to download free software and create a site which provides its citizens access to the government data for innovation, economic development and transparency. An Indian delegation from National Informatics Centre visited Kigali in October 2012 to discuss the implementation of the trilateral initiative with their Rwandan counterparts.

Training

India is seen as a destination for quality and affordable education by Rwandans. In 2011 alone, around 700 Rwandan students joined Indian universities. Indian teachers serve various institutions in Rwanda, including the Kigali Institute of Science & Technology (KIST) and the Butare University. KIST and the Vellore Institute of Technology (VIT) signed an MOU in 2001 to facilitate training of KIST faculty members in VIT and deputation of teachers from VIT to KIST. VIT also provides education to Rwandan students at its institute in undergraduate, postgraduate and IT courses as per an MOU with the Ministry of Education, Science, Technology and Scientific Research, Government of Rwanda since 2002.

The Government of India offers scholarships and fellowships to Rwandans from the Government and private sector to enable them to pursue under-graduate, graduate, post-graduate and research courses in India. India offers 53 scholarships every year to Rwanda under different schemes.

Training courses in highly specialised areas are also conducted for officers of public institutions. During 2011, Rwandan officials participated in training programmes in the fields of Operation & Maintenance of Hydroelectric Power stations, ICT, Disaster Management, Agriculture and Drug Law Enforcement.

India's effort to contribute in process of Rwanda's Capacity Building and Human Resource Development is well appreciated by Rwanda.

Burundi

India's engagement with Burundi is at three levels viz. at the African Union (AU) level, at level of the Regional Economic Communities (RECs) and at the bilateral level.

Moreover, India's engagement with Burundi has been consultative, response-based and focused on developing Burundian capacities and human capital. Indian assistance to Burundi has been guided mainly by the announcements made by India at the India-Africa Forum Summits in 2008 and 2009.

Following the first India Africa Forum Summit (IAFS-I) in 2008, Burundi was nominated by the AU to host the India-Africa Institute of Educational Planning and Administration (IAIEPA), one of the 5 institutes offered by India at the Pan-Africa level. The institute is mandated to strengthen the capacities in the region in the sector of education. The Indian implementing agency National University of Education Planning & Administration (NUEPA) is likely to start the first courses at the IAIEPA soon.

Under IAFS-I, India offered eight Vocational Training Centres (VTCs); one each to the eight RECs. Burundi was nominated as one of the countries to host the VTC. The centre will impart vocational training to people from the region to enable them to be gainfully employed or become entrepreneurs. This again is one of the Indian efforts towards human resource development in Africa. The Indian implementing agency, National Small Industries Corporation (NSIC) and the Burundian Ministry for Primary and Secondary Education, Crafts and Vocational Training and Literacy are finalizing the finer details.

At the second India-Africa Forum Summit (IAFS-II) in Government of India announced 40 biomass gasifier systems, out of which a cluster bio-mass gasifier system is being established in Burundi. These are expected to provide low cost sustainable electricity in villages by powering a gas engine. A team of experts from the implementing agency in India is expected to visit Burundi soon to undertake feasibility studies for the project.

At IAFS-II, India also offered, among other things, eight Farm Science Centres (FSCs), one each for the 8 RECs. FSC is an innovative institution of the Indian Council of Agriculture Research (ICAR) which has played a pivotal role in application of technology at farm levels in India since 1974. Burundi has been selected by the East African Community for hosting one such FSC. A team from India would be visiting Burundi soon for inspection of the sites proposed by Burundi side for setting- up the centre.

In addition to the above institutions, a tele-medical centre and a tele-education centre have been set up in Bujumbura in 2010 under the Pan-African E-Network Project. The project aims to provide quality and real-time medical care and education from India at a fraction of cost. The project is functioning successfully.

Government of India has extended a Line of Credit of US$ 80 million for the 20MW Kabu hydro-electric project. In this regard, an agreement between the EXIM Bank of India and the Government of Burundi was signed in May, 2011. H.E. Mr. Gervais Rufyikiri, Vice President of Burundi laid the foundation stone for the Kabu HEP in Cibitoke Province on 30th August, 2012.

Training: India is seen as a destination for quality and affordable education by Burundians. The Government of India offers scholarships and fellowships to Burundians from the Government and private sector to enable them to pursue under-graduate, graduate, post-graduate and research courses in India. Training courses in highly specialised areas are also conducted for officers of public institutions. India offers 40 scholarships every year to Burundi under different schemes.

Rationale of Development Assistance

No doubt the transfers from India to its African partners were small in the first three or four decades of these programmes' existence, and although India's development assistance to Africa is still insignificant in financial terms, it has been boosted massively over the last few years. However, there were more reasons: India's competition with China played a major role in setting up the summit[14], and it was also seen as a way to reinvent and rejuvenate an old relationship between India and Africa and thereby influence the global political and economic agenda. Just as important, however, was India's aim to diversify its energy resources (India currently imports twenty percent of its oil imports from Africa (eleven percent from Nigeria)), create market access for Indian products and pave ways for Indian investments in Africa (Africa- Asia Confidential, 2008; Cherian, 2008).

During the last decade India's development aid contribution and activities have increased manifold. Current trends suggest that India could become a net exporter of aid in the next few years while this transformation is being driven by a combination of factors, including India's self-conscious role as an emerging power, its competition with other players for political influence and energy resources, and the rapid growth of its economy, including both its non-profit and private sectors. In a changing global scenario a large number of African countries, including the countries in East Africa, desire to develop closer ties with India on economic, educational, scientific, social, technological and political front. During the two Africa-Indian Summits Africa and India laid the foundations for a stronger development-centric partnership revolving around capacity building, HRD, training and trade.

Besides the expected benefits from India's development cooperation for African countries there also remain some challenges and risks. India's development cooperation policy approach is clearly distinct from the OECD/DAC approach, the principles of non-interference and mutual respect for sovereignty remaining major features

The major features of India's development co-operation are the affirmation of mutual interest, and the rejection of conditionality as a modality for transacting development co-operation. The Indian approach treats recipients of its assistance as development partners and links development co-operation with the demonstration of solidarity at a political level. Development partners in turn share a common history of mutual co-operation grounded in political solidarity typically dating back to the Cold War period. This co-operation was not based on resource transfers but rather on experience and knowledge sharing. As India becomes an emerging economy the financial measurement of its co-operation becomes comparable to that of the aid giving countries, but the fact remains that India's engagement with development partners is different in motivation, intent and history from that of the aid givers.

Comparison with Chinese

Parallels are often drawn between India and China's development partnership initiatives with Africa. Indeed, their trade with Africa has grown over the years compared to European partners. It is generally stated that for both India and China, access to natural resources and especially oil is the main driver in their development assistance programmes.

There are important differences though. India's assistance in material terms is far less than China. Besides, unlike China's investment in Africa, which is led by state-owned companies, Indian investment is mainly driven by the private sector. In another contrast with Chinese companies, India hires local labourers while many Chinese companies bring Chinese labourers to their projects in East Africa.

Indian officials admit that China's aid-for-oil strategy, which involves extension of soft loans for massive infrastructure projects in return for oil, helped Beijing secure deals in its favour. India is unable to match the aid the Chinese offered, which underscores the need for an approach that built on India's strengths, which ultimately resulted in India focusing on capacity building in East Africa.

Policy options

Development assistance is an important tool for meeting India's strategic and foreign policy goals. However, in case of Africa in general and East Africa in particular, India is yet to evolve mechanisms for effective deployment to those ends. What has not always worked as well is the pace of implementation of many Indian projects in East Africa. It is true that as democratic country consultations and building consensus takes time. Sometimes overly strong bureaucracy takes too literally its obligation to act as a check and balance on decision making. There is an undoubted need however for more careful management and audit of disbursements made through the governments lines of credit for Africa. In 2009 several reports appeared of questionable transactions relating to the export of rice at subsidized prices to several countries. Given that LOC amount to considerable sums of money- more than 5 billion- there is a fundamental need for greater transparency in the allocation of funds, the choice of projects, the drawing up of the requirements and selection of contractors. This should not allow to slow the process down, but it is essential. India's relation with East Africa should not be reduced in the eyes of current development policy towards East Africa both at the regional and bilateral level which rests on three planks: technical support, training programmes led by ITEC and project based support programmes. It is undeniable that there are not only limited ties between foreign policy objectives and development cooperation, but also linkages between three planks which need strengthening.

Assessment

Returning to the questions posed at the beginning of this chapter, the significant issue is whether India is shaping a new development discourse in Africa including East Africa. Until now much of the discourse has been preoccupied by China's increasing engagements across the continent, with some analysts suggest that a 'Beijing Consensus' could replace the Washington Consensus, on which the western model for developing countries is based. India on its part, differentiates its development model from that of West and sees its engagements in East Africa as well as other parts of Africa, to be based on south-south framework. India and China are generally clubbed together as far as development model is concerned, but India follows an independent trajectory based on its foreign policy priorities, experiences and capabilities. This is perhaps what even Prime Minister Manmohan Singh referred to in his remark in the India-Africa Summit in 2008, though it is not clear from India's policy on Africa in general as to how its engagement with the African states including those of East Africa will be different.

What is required, therefore, is an understanding of the inter-sections between India's domestic priorities and its current foreign policy ambitions and how these correspond to the common interests around East Africa's sustainable development project. So far it seems that India is on a global offensive to encourage its private sector to invest in African countries including East Africa. This is revitalizing the domestic economy through the private sector's pursuit of market opportunities and pushing India up at global stage. But how does Africa and East Africa in particular fit into this paradigm?

It is apparent that India is pursuing a policy of trade, training and technology in respect of East Africa. This is infused with a development-centric approach that is aimed at enhancing trade, transferring technology, capacity building and human resource development. The government believes that this gives India a comparative advantage over other actors in East Africa. India boasts strong scientific research and development capacity, which has produced cost-effective technology, and its growing presence on the region means that East Africans can potentially access such technology. Moreover the production in India of cheap generic drugs to combat preventable diseases, such as malaria, TB, cholera and yellow fever, and anti-retrovirals to treat HIV/AIDS, is also seen as a way to support improvements to East Africa's public health systems.

At the same time India believes that it can share with East Africa its experience in renewable energy techniques, such as the solar power engineering project in Ethiopia, Kenya, Rwanda and Tanzania, where small medium and micro-enterprise development and microfinance prospects are being discussed in respect of rural development projects. India is also increasing the level of scientific cooperation by creating post-doctoral scholarships for East African students to study at its prestigious science and engineering colleges and universities. Finally, the setting up of vocational training centres to train East African artisans and create opportunities for East African skills to be developed in sectors like call centre programmes and agricultural development is ongoing.

Although all these developments point to an India that is increasingly aware of the need to improve the material standards of East African people in order that the region's economic leverage can increase, India-East Africa engagement is not without challenges. One of the major challenges the effectiveness of the development measures that India has undertaken. It is questioned on the basis of procedural hindrances, implementation gap, time and cost overrun and visibility deficit, and most importantly, their relevance to developmental needs and priorities of the target groups. What is important to gauge is whether the initiatives that India has been undertaking is making change in the lives of the people. Synergizing the collective interests of the people of India and East Africa remain a challenge particularly in the context of trade and investment.

Another issue is India's constant referral to the Indian diaspora in East Africa, which it sees as an important link to the continent and a natural justification for developing closer political and economic ties. But India has in fact neglected the diaspora in East Africa, particularly when racial tensions played themselves out in Uganda. What underpins the connection to the diaspora is a class-driven project in which the economic elites with political connections are those with whom the government engages. As much as the East African Indian community recognises its ancestral roots, it does not express a strong political and economic affinity with India. It is primarily the economic elites who enjoy a prosperous relationship with India.

More controversial is land acquisition. Indian firms invested almost $3 billion in farm acquisitions for commercial food crops and biofuels production between 2007 and 2010.[15] In African countries including East Africa, African and Indian authorities claim that such acquisitions are part of the transfer of skills and expertise in technology, but some consternation has been expressed by those who see these investments as mainly aimed at ensuring India's food security by tapping into East Africa's bread baskets. This, indeed, raises concern about the East African countries, food sovereignty, about the protection of land rights of subsistence farmers and about the displacement of farmers from their land. Given the sensitive nature of this commercial agricultural investment, India has faced criticism of engaging in a 21st century land grab. Though India's development-centric approach has been welcomed by Africans, it is generally emphasized by Africans that India should be a stakeholder and not a shareholder in the region's development.[16]

Ultimately, it is how East African countries themselves define their relationships with India that will determine whether New Delhi is a development partner. Currently, India's political and economic engagement reflects both its development objectives and its clearly corporate interest in the region. East African states do not have to allow this relationship to mirror the 19th century scramble for resources, and India will have to leverage the international milieu to ensure that it benefits. This will require bold leadership and pragmatic decision making: something that Indian diplomats seem to be taking seriously by making themselves more visible and accessible to their East African counterparts.

During his tour, Vice-President Hamid Ansari's comments to the media made clear the state's intent:

> The direction in which the Indian economy is going, the major role will be played; by the private sector, especially in industrial development. Local employment will be generated. It doesn't make economic sense to take work force from India because it comes with liabilities. When we go for an investment venture, we don't go with the idea of imposing our work force or employment of Indians per se. We seek to limit ourselves to management and financial control of enterprises having an Indian element. (IANS 2010)[17]

If this is the case, then African commentator; activists and social movements need to be tracking the Indian footprint in East Africa. The question that should be asked is whether India, indeed, offers something different from other external players, or is it more of the same? Moreover, can this be assumed that because India's involvement in East Africa is not in the same league as that of emerging powers or other actors from the global North one can afford to become blind sided by the cliche that it does business differently. One can argue that India's engagement and approach is based on its own experiences, which it is willing to share.

India's ambitions and interest in East Africa till now has not aroused the same criticism as those of China, but in the end one need to ask whether they cater to the interest of locals or to the elite class. It is important that India is mindful of the impact such patterns have on people's livelihoods, land rights, long-term skilled employment, and environmental justice. Therefore the Indian government would do well to learn the lessons experienced by other actors in the East African market and landscape: 'the type of sensitivities, threats and backlashes that are present and can arise; and how to diffuse these situations before they become the victims of their own self-confidence. The political and economic elites in the Indian diaspora and among East Africa's ruling class are only two sets of stakeholders. The ordinary people, civil society groups and others that fall outside this ambit must be consulted if India truly wants to be a different development partner to East African countries.

Conclusion

To sum up, India has acknowledged the importance of East African countries in its Africa policy. Hence, collaborations with East African countries have recently been scaled-up and publicized massively. India's development assistance, however, is still small in terms of funds transferred, but it is not insignificant as it may create a new platform for South-South dialogue and it is framed as a partnership between equal partners, which may enhance the developmental aspect of it. Moreover, it tends to focus on trade-related issues. India's development assistance is totally linked to India's own capabilities and its interests in East Africa. It is a combination of tied project aid and scholarships and it mainly targets those East African countries rich in resource or rich in Indian diaspora.

More problematically, like China, India lacks an official definition of what counts as development assistance. The official records of development assistance kept, either by the Ministry of External Affairs or the Ministry of Finance are not made public. However, with the creation of the Development Partnership Administration (DPA) within MEA, efforts are being made to make all the forms of assistance streamlined and issues of adhocism addressed with emphasis given to transparency and evaluation.

The India Development Initiative effort is a tool to strengthen south-south cooperation and support the national efforts of developing countries while promoting India's long-term interests. "India's exports to Africa have risen to US $3.8 billion and imports are $2.2 billion. In the past six months, they have surged 32 percent. Survey shows that 5 of the 10 fastest growing economies in the world are in Africa." The EXIM Bank provides advisory services to facilitate the participation of Indian companies in trade with East Africa. It has tied up with the AFDB and other financial institutions and has taken part in institution building processes in East African countries and in various development projects. However, it has to be ensured that all these development initiatives are efficiently managed with constant monitoring and periodic evaluation, so that they are effective on ground.

Endnotes

1.   Sachin Chaturvedi, Thomas Fues, Elizabeth Sidropolous (ED), Development Cooperation and Emerging Powers, Zed Books, London, 2012.

2.   Peter Kragelund, The Potential Role of Non Traditional Donors in Africa, Issue Paper no.11, International Centre for Trade and Sustainable Development.

3.   Kragelund, 2008; Price, 2004.

4.   Chanan, 2009.

5.   India in Africa Changing Geographies of Power.

6.   Jobelius 2007; Kragelund 2008; Rowlands 2008.

7.   Sachin Chaturvedi, Thomas Fues, Elizabeth Sidropolous (ED), Development Cooperation and Emerging Powers, Zed Books, London, 2012, p177

68   *India's Engagement with East Africa: Opportunities and Challenges*

8. Katti et al 2009; Sinha 2010.

9. Sashi Tharoor, Familiar Lands and Uncharted Territories, Pax Indica, p 257; Penguin BooksIndia, 2012.

10. Katti et al 2009

11. Shashi Tharoor, p 256.

12. Shashi Tharoor, p 261.

13. http://paepard.blogspot.com/2011/05/india-africa-to-cooperate-for html

14. Chanana, D. (2009) 'India as an emerging donor', Economic and Political Weekly, vol. 44, no. 12

15. Vashisht, Dinkor (2010) 'India's Punjabi farmers investigate farming in Africa', African Agriculture, 26 July, http://www.africanagricultureblog.com/2010/07/ondias-punjabi-farmers-investigatt.htm , accessed on 24th February, 2011.

16. India-Africa Summit (2008) 'Address by Prime Minister Manmohan Singh to the first India-Africa Summit', April, http://pib.nic.in/releaseirelease.asp?relid=37177, accessed 24 February 2011.

17. IANS (2010) 'India's private sector will power Africa thrust: Vice President', 12 January, http://www.thaindian.com/newsportal/business/indias-private-sector-will-power-aErica-thrust-vice-president-lead_100302698html accessed on 15 February 2011

Chapter - 3

India –East Africa Economic Linkages: Role of Indian Private Sector

Introduction

The exponential growth of trade and investment linkages between India and East Africa in the recent years, with a range of initiatives- many of them private sector led, has injected a new momentum to the historical relations. Though the trade relations between East Africa and India are centuries old, yet according to many analysts and businessmen East African nations are engaged with a renewed wave of Indian exporters in sectors in which Indian products are able to compete on price and adapt to local conditions. India is now one of the top five foreign investors in East African countries such as Kenya, Mozambique and Tanzania. Private-sector companies are the main drivers of India's investments, unlike China where investments are predominantly state-driven, covering sectors such as telecommunications, agriculture, hotels, mining, rail and road infrastructure and pharmaceuticals. Indian companies namely Kirloskar Brothers Limited, the Tata Group, Mahindra and Mahindra, Bharti Airtel, Fortis, Escort and Apollo are increasingly seeking to expand their business activities and diversify their markets in the East Africa region. In sectors such as agriculture, pharmaceuticals and health, IT & telecoms and infrastructure, Indian investment in East Africa has increased significantly in recent years. This chapter will be exploring the economic linkages between India and East African countries, with emphasis on the role of private sectors and focus on factors promoting the relations, the emerging sectors of cooperation and the challenges.

Factors promoting Economic Linkages

This dramatic growth of the Indian private sector in East Africa, particularly after the India Africa Summit in the year 2008, has been due to various factors. Significantly, it is due to initiatives taken up by the

Confederation of Indian Industries (CII), Exim Bank of India and the heads of major Indian companies at the broader level of promoting India-Africa partnership. Between 2004 and 2014, the CII and Exim Bank have jointly organised seven major events that brought together key Indian and African private sector organisations and government representatives, including East African countries, to discuss and review the progress made in deepening economic engagement between India and Africa in general and East Africa in particular[1]. Government-to-government involvement has also grown following the first India-Africa Forum Summit in New Delhi in 2008 and in Addis Ababa in 2011. Lines of Credit offered by India to African countries have also contributed to promotion of economic ties. Around 52 percent of India Exim Bank's global lines of credit have been offered to African countries and to date, a sizeable percentage has been focused on infrastructure (hydropower, rural electrification and railway rehabilitation) and on agriculture.

In addition, to the Indian private sector, Indian state-owned corporations, such as the Indian Telecom Industries, Rail India Technical and Economic Services (Rites), Konkan Railways, the ONGC and many others have also been very active in the extractive sector as well as in large-scale construction projects, such as roads, railways, telecommunications and the building construction sectors. For example, although Rites and IRCON, the two large state-owned infrastructure and engineering companies have been engaged in construction of rail networks and the leasing of locomotives in Sudan, Tanzania, Kenya and Mozambique, companies such as Kalapataru Power Transmission Ltd. have secured major contracts to build power transmission sites. In general, the state-owned enterprises work very closely with the Indian private enterprise and operators in both sectors drawing a great deal of support from the Exim Bank through its LoC programme.

The Exim Bank has been a key institution and that has played a critical role in facilitating the entry of Indian private sector companies into Africa, including the financing of major capital projects on the continent[2]. It has done this through its LOCs to East African governments, parastatal boards, regional groups such as the Eastern and Southern African Trade and Development Bank, and the East Africa Development Bank to promote Indian exports and consultancy services to East Africa.[3] Examples of funded projects in East Africa executed by Indian companies include: supply of pharmaceuticals (Uganda); building of transmission lines

(Kenya); telecom projects; a railway construction project (Tanzania); and a sewerage study (Ethiopia).[4] The increasing volume of LoCs to individual East African countries, and regional groups by the Exim Bank, indicates a private sector-led engagement of India and East Africa. But whether it will lead to a sustainable development of East Africa, remains a question. For India it is important to balance credits for promoting export of Indian goods and LoCs for supporting Indian investment aimed at East African growth and development, in the long term. The OECD, however, has been extremely critical of India as well as China with regard to their approach to trade with Africa in general and East Africa in particular, arguing that both the Asian giants are mainly interested in securing raw materials and energy from Africa and finding new markets for their cheap goods and services. Because this could lead to 'Dutch disease' in African countries including East Africa, it is not to Africa's advantage in the long term[5]. This conclusion has already been assigned to Chinese investments in Africa and India will not be able to escape the same criticism if it fails to heed East African concerns.

In addition to providing export credits, the Exim Bank has bought equity stake in the East Africa Export-Import Bank, the West African Development Bank and the Development Bank of Zambia. It also has a strong relationship with the African Development Bank (AFDB), and as a non-regional member of this bank has been able to assist Indian companies to bid successfully in AFDB-financed infrastructure projects in East Africa. It also influences private sector development in East Africa through its consultancy and advisory services to numerous East African governments and the World Bank Group, resulting in the participation of Indian companies in projects financed by the International Finance Corporation under its Africa project development facility, the Africa Enterprise Fund and the Technical Assistance and Trust Fund in a number of African countries.[6]

Regionally the East Africa community (Kenya, Uganda, Tanzania, Rwanda and Burundi) being in the proximity of Indian Ocean, provides immense opportunities for trade and investment. In the words of Ambassador Juma V Mwapachi, Secretary General, East African Community (EAC) Secretariat, Tanzania, 'market access is extremely important, as it lies at the heart of economic engagement and integration in the world and it opens up new economic vistas for bolstering trade. Market expansion is also important because of the reason that it enables structuring economic relations with other economic blocks and countries.'

The regional approach of development in Africa has made India to fit into this framework and one may observe that there is a perceptible shift in India's approach to the region. East African Community's collective engagement with Indian investors is beneficial for East Africa's development on the one side and the Indian industry on the other side. Mr. Sanjay Kirloskar, Chairman Kirloskar Brothers Ltd in India –Africa conclave has highlighted that 'a regional approach will give the member states greater opportunities to attract foreign investments. In the case of Africa, regionalism has received special attention as a result of growing fears of African marginalization. The process of creating a free trade area that incorporates the East African Community, the Common Market for Eastern and Southern Africa, and the Southern African Development Community is underway — bringing together nearly 600 million people into a single market. Such a development will have a major bearing on India-Africa economic exchanges. There are also important developments within the existing regional markets' (CII Conclave, April 2009).

India can play a catalytic role in furthering the regional economic integrative forces. Providing an "in-house experience", Mr Obadiah K Mbaya, Chairman, IDB Capital Ltd, Kenya, said his country has benefited significantly from the Government of India Line of Credit (LOC). Kenya has received the last LoC in 2003 and expressed hope that a new LOC will be made available to Kenya soon. The LoCs have helped the Kenyan government in its endeavour to facilitate easy financing to industry, transfer of technology, value addition of primary commodities, employment generation, greater international trade and bilateral cooperation with India. The LoCs also helped India to increase its exports to Kenya.' (CII Conclave, April 2009). The objective will not just be a quantitative increase in trade and investments; it will also aim at a qualitative enhancement (through transfer of technology) of East Africa's economic competitiveness and technology capabilities. It is one of the cutting-edge differences between India's relationship as an emerging power with East Africa as compare to traditional partners'.

Kenya, Uganda and Tanzania as member states of EAC are working on eliminating non-tariff barriers and modernizing infrastructure, integrating their capital markets, and generally harmonizing their key policies and regulations to reduce the costs of doing business with the international community. The approach of Indian investors in Kenya, Uganda or Tanzania opens the gate to the entire East African regional market. The infrastructure development in EAC has been observed during my visits to these countries in the early months of 2009.

The institutional entrepreneurship in East Africa is represented through CII, FICCI, EXIM (BANK), IOR-ARC, and Focus Africa. Different turnkey contracts are working in Tanzania, Uganda and others. It enables import of Indian equipment and technology on deferred credit terms extended through EXIM Bank, PTA Bank, BOAD, EADB and EBID. Joint Ventures of Indian companies engage in East Africa through Line of Credit. A visible change in perception with access to greater knowledge of the region has helped in promoting economic relations between the Indian industry members and the East African countries. CII effort is to develop a long term sustainable relationship with the private sector in the East African countries.

India–Africa Business conclave has been able to foster greater economic linkages between both sides. The participants in these conclaves have been remarked by huge participation of African Indian delegates, wherein various projects worth billions, in technology, agriculture, human resources and energy in the East Africa region have been discussed [7]. All the institutions played an active role during conclaves and sponsored it as per their capacities. CII Africa Committee has Institutional Agreements with Africa's Small and Medium Enterprise (SME) and signed Memorandum of Understanding (MoU) in the fields of soap plan, water management and infrastructure related projects during the 5th Conclave. A strong structure that supports a continuing dialogue, transparent access to opportunities, interaction with the government and the African Heads of Missions has been institutionalized in Conclaves.

Various measures on the part of India has led to promotion trade between India and East African states. For instance India-Tanzania bilateral trade is increasing in terms of volume. India's export touches US$ 237.02 million and import of US$ 56.56 million (2006 estimate). The principal commodities of exports deals with mineral fuels, pharmaceuticals, cotton textiles, engineering goods, iron & steel, motor vehicles, consumer goods and garments. The import works in raw cashew nuts, gemstones, raw cotton, pulses and timber. The trade between Tanzania and India has increased in the past few years and now stands at over $750 million a year before being expected to increase further in the next few years. Tanzania has joined the India-Africa duty-free tariff preference scheme that was announced during India-Africa Forum Summit in 2008. India is ranked among the top three countries in both the export and import categories with Tanzania.[8]

Hence overall, India is playing to its strengths in East Africa. As stated earlier, Indian companies are active in agriculture, ICT and communications infrastructure, and health sectors. Indian expertise in communications has been coupled with East Africa's need for rapid growth in, mobile phone and internet infrastructure. In 2010, the Indian telecoms company Bharti Airtel announced a USD 10.7bn deal to purchase the African operations of Zain Telecommunications, the largest Indian investment on the continent to date.

India has been seen as a counterbalance to China in East Africa. Although investment is smaller in scale, a much longer historical presence of an Indian diaspora in East Africa has enabled smoother and less controversial economic involvement in East Africa than is the case for China. The key for East African governments will be how they manage their emerging economic partners to ensure maximum economic development impact. In this sense, foreign investment objectives and East African development aims are aligned: only continued economic development in East Africa will allow for further deepening of trade and investment relationships.[9]

Investment in Kenya

Of the $136 million of Indian FDI into Kenya between 2007 and 2011, nearly 89 percent focused on the manufacturing sector. Indian corporate giant Tata Chemical's soda ash manufacturing plant in Kenya's Lake Magadi region – valued at about $97 million – is one of the biggest drivers of this investment. The plant, the largest of its kind in Africa, is also one of Kenya's leading exporters. Rather than producing raw products for export back to Tata's operations on the subcontinent, Magadi exports regionally within Africa, to the Middle East and to Southeast Asia. Consumers along the Indian Ocean account for 95 percent of the plant's annual exports.[10]

Kenya and India share a history, having both been British colonies. Indeed, Kenya hosts an Indian expatriate population of about 100,000, which, despite being part of a population of approximately 34 million, operates nearly 75 percent of successful retail operations in the country, according to Reserve Bank of India and Kenyan High Commission statistics. Kenya, the regional financial center, is also a key export market for Indian goods, consuming $1.7 billion worth of Indian exports in 2011. Given its improving road infrastructure, built in part by Indian and Chinese construction firms, and the fact that it serves as a regional air and rail hub, Kenya offers India export access to Central African states, most notably Ethiopia and Uganda.[11]

Kenya has called upon Indian entrepreneurs to explore investment opportunities in the areas of textiles, fertilizers, pesticides and tyres. Kenya offers various benefits to investors including a liberal economic regime, cheap labour, investment guarantee and protection, good market access to developed countries. Indian entrepreneurs to look at setting up units in Kenya's export processing zones in the area of textiles and take advantage of the duty-free and quota-free access to the US provided under the Africa Growth Opportunities Act (AGOA). There is a need for diversification of trade between India and Kenya in both volume and value terms

Kenya signed a new bilateral agreement with India, geared towards advancing trade, investment and technical cooperation on 22nd December 2008. India-Kenya Joint Trade Committee (JTC) touches on various sectors of economy of both countries to enhance trade, investment and technical cooperation between the two countries. The agreement further stated that in order to enhance competitiveness in the agricultural sector, the Indian National Research and Development Corporation (NRDC) would assist Kenya in value addition, packaging and technological interventions to enhance agricultural output. Regarding lines of credit, the Kenyan delegation expressed interest in accessing Lines of Credit (LoC) for several sectors including cooperation in trade and investment in the Export Processing Zones, joint venture investment in textile sector, co-operation in tea and coffee sectors, targeting process technology and research and development. Furthermore, agreement was reached on development of infrastructure projects with emphasis on Build Operate Transfer (BoT), co-operation in business process outsourcing, administration of standards, co-operation in energy efficiency and conservation, bilateral investment promotion and protection agreement.

Investment in Uganda

Like neighbouring Rwanda and the Democratic Republic of the Congo, Uganda has experienced strong economic growth since about 2000 due in part to the performance of its agricultural sectors but also due to increased outside investment targeting the region's mineral wealth. Such investment is a result of Uganda's attractive investment climate and good economic governance. Gold, diamonds and coltan — a critical mineral component in many high-tech devices — are found in abundance in the region, though more so in bordering states. As in Kenya, India's investments in Uganda extend beyond resource acquisition. Several major Indian corporations, including Bharti Airtel and the Bank of Baroda (India's largest public sector lender), have set up operations in Uganda, hoping to profit from the expansion of the local economy. Service-sector investment has also increased through a joint venture between India's Devyani International and Kenya's Sameer Investments Ltd. that attracted more than $25 million of investment in local hotels and restaurants between 2008 and 2010 alone.

Uganda's and Kenya's import and export infrastructure are intricately linked, especially along the Lake Victoria corridor. Because of this, Uganda, like Kenya, enables Indian investors to increase their involvement in the economies of neighbouring countries. Indian investment in Central Africa has lagged behind that of Europe and China, whose investors have been aggressively seeking access to local resources. As India's overall economic growth slows and future development is increasingly constrained by poor infrastructure, Uganda's high GDP growth (averaging about 7 percent a year since 2000) and growing educated labour force could provide Indian corporations with alternative high-growth markets.

Investment in Tanzania

Tanzania's investment promotion agencies are inviting Indian investors into the country, promising unrivalled supportive business environment.[12] It is welcoming Indian investors to invest under Special Economic Zones (SEZ) and the incentive rich Export Processing Zones (EPZ), and there are the numbers of business incentives that investors stand to enjoy under the SEZ/EPZ programmes. The government, through its business promotion agencies, is determined to address the impediments that still haunt investors in the country.

Recent years have seen consistent business growth between these two countries, reaching 1.7 billion US dollars in 2011, and noting that India is among the four top trading partners of Tanzania. Tanzania's exports to India are reportedly rising faster than India's to Tanzania, bridging the trade gap. India's imports from Tanzania reached almost half a billion US dollars in 2012.

The three good reasons to invest in Tanzania are (i) Market Access; (ii) Resources and opportunities; and (iii) Stability and related factors. Tanzania has no shortage of opportunities – in tourism, in agriculture, in energy. The political maturity of the country and its economic stability are major strengths that investors can rely on. With some serious attention to infrastructure, the Government could ensure that the country's potential becomes reality. Foreign ownership up to 100 percent is allowed in infrastructure investment, including highway construction, bridges, telecommunication, airports, railways, water distribution and power generation.

Indian Prime Minister Manmohan Singh, visit to Tanzania in 2011, unveiled a handsome grants package for the nation. This included $ 191 million in lines of credit and grants for a slew of development projects and a 300-bed hospital to be set up in capital Dar-es-Salaam. The super specialty facility will be set up by Apollo Hospitals within the next two years. Tanzanian President Jakaya Kikwete expressed hope that Apollo could set up five more hospitals in his country in the future. Two more pacts were signed after wide- ranging talks between Singh and Kikwete. The two nations signed a double taxation avoidance agreement to promote investment, besides another pact to promote development of small-scale industries in Tanzania and India. But Kikwete sought more support from New Delhi to boost its economy and social sector, describing the $ 1.3-billion investment by India till now as "too little". He had said "India has surplus capital. Tanzania wants more Indian investments in agriculture, health, education and IT and communication sectors." [13]

The PM agreed with his host. "India is ready to partner Tanzania in its nation- building efforts. India will focus on areas such as agriculture, small and medium industries, healthcare and human resource development."[14] Indian investment and technology can help Tanzania become an industrial and technological hub of East Africa and its engine of growth.

The major highlight of the visit was (i) $ 191 million in lines of credit and grants for development projects (This includes $ 180 million for water supply projects in Tanzania, $ 10 million for capacity building projects in the social & educational sectors and $ 1 million for development); (ii) A 300- bed hospital to be set up by the Apollo group in Dar-es-Salaam (iii) Signing of a double taxation avoidance agreement to promote greater investment; (iv) A pact to promote small- scale industries has also been signed.[15]

Sector wise Analysis

Agriculture Sector

Agriculture is vital for the development goals of promoting growth and reducing poverty in Africa. Agriculture supports the livelihoods of 80 percent of the African population, provides employment for about 60 percent of the economically active population, and for about 70 percent of the poorest people on the continent. The global financial and food crises have brought agriculture into sharp focus, demonstrating that poverty and food insecurity goes hand in hand. Agricultural growth is a proven driver of poverty reduction in agriculture based economy. When agriculture stimulates growth in Africa, the growth is twice as effective in reducing poverty as growth based in other sectors.

Today, East Africa is the hub of natural resources with leading world powers eyeing the region. Only an average 3 percent of cultivatable land in Africa is being used now, which is not sufficient to feed the entire population of East Africa. It is imperative to incorporate the development of the agriculture sector as a prerequisite to an East African country's progress and overall prosperity. Africa agriculture today is one of the most under capitalized in the world. Only seven percent of the arable land in Africa is irrigated, compared to 40 percent in Asia. The use of the fertilizer per hectare by African farmers is far lower than that used by the Asian farmers the Asian farmers. The number of tractors per 1000 ha of arable land is three times greater in Asia and eight times greater in Latin America than in Africa. Similarly, road densities are more than 2.5 times higher in Latin America and 6 times higher in Asia than in Africa. With regard to innovations, African institutions of agricultural higher education, research and extension are poorly staffed, ill equipped and under-funded. This is very much the situation in East Africa [16]

As a result of this severe under-capitalization, the rural landscape in East Africa is still marked by small holder subsistence farms, low technology and weak knowledge-based agricultural production systems, owing to the lack of development and widespread use of appropriate technologies and to extreme paucity in basic support infrastructure. The combined effects of these features include stagnating or declining agricultural productivity, weak backward and forward linkages between agriculture and other sectors, loss of competitiveness in world markets, increased food insecurity and natural resource and environmental degradation. The problem is further compounded by other global level challenges, such as commodity price volatility and protectionist policies and domestic agricultural subsidies by the OECD countries.[17] For highly import-dependent countries of East Africa, with limited foreign exchange, the import of food at high costs is not a feasible choice. Any escalation in prices leads to decreasing of purchasing power, which in turn affects food security and nutrition levels. Food availability is, therefore, pressing concern to the East Africa region.

However, despite the challenges of food insecurity, the region has immense potential for agricultural transformation. It is believed by the African leaders that although the arable land currently under cultivation in Africa is very less, it has the potential to become the food basket of the world. The Comprehensive African Agriculture Development Programme (CAADP), under the aegis of the New Partnership for Africa's Development (NEPAD), has identified the agriculture sector as an "engine of growth" and a potential "sustainable solution to hunger and poverty in Africa".

As a region East Africa is fertile and has abundance of water, consisting of rivers and lakes. It needs water pumping system and water management techniques. The requirement is for changing the production pattern in agriculture with the use of better seed technology, irrigation, scientific techniques and infrastructure. There is also need for research in areas of water management and water harvesting to strengthen their agriculture set up. Besides each country has its uniqueness in its agricultural potential and policies. For instance in Uganda agro processing can improve the livelihood of low income groups as it produces cereals, root crops, coffee, tea, livestock, fish and forestry. There is a lot of scope for business in processed agro products. India and East Africa have started quota free trade and thus Ugandan products will be sold duty free in India. The linkage potential in the plantation and agro industry includes:

- Outsourcing the field operations including seed bed preparation.

- Supply of produce to processors.

- Maintenance of machinery.

This agro industry needs strong infrastructure such as roads, railway, etc. in Uganda. It requires a more efficient railways network to connect Kenya, Tanzania and Rwanda. This is a very important area of investment for Indian investors. Tanzania in the other hand is known as the spice islands, It offers investment opportunities in horticulture and floriculture, agro processing, fruit processing & canning, cloves, cinnamon, cardamom, nutmeg, black pepper, chilies, etc. likewise other countries have their distinctive agrarian nature and relations, which offers opportunities

Realising the potential of their land assets and the relevance of Indian experience in the agriculture sector, the leaders in East Africa believe that to realise the potential of their land, they need to forge partnerships and seek investments with India to overcome severe problems of under-capitalisation, infrastructure and production pattern. The agriculture sector can get an immense impetus through foreign direct investment based on partnership and mutual reciprocity and thus help create "land as assets". In this context therefore Indian private sectors investments stands significant. It has the potential to address the critical gaps in the basic infrastructure such as irrigation facilities, technological up gradation, rural electrification, roads and waterways and capacity building.

At the April 9, 2008 India-Africa Forum Summit held at New Delhi, the President of Tanzania and former chairperson of the AU, Jakaya Mrisho Kikwete, voiced Africa's concern for food security and urged India to invest in capacity building in this crucial sector. He underlined that "If we are able to increase productivity in African agriculture, Africa would not only be able to feed itself, but will have huge surpluses to sell to the world. India has the technology and the skills, which, if made available to Africa, will certainly help it, implement the African Green Revolution,"

The India-Africa Framework for Cooperation that was adopted jointly at the end of the India-Africa Forum Summit 2008, identified the development of sustainable agriculture as a key priority in the burgeoning partnership between India and Africa. "Africa and India agree that agricultural development is an effective approach to ensure food security, eradicating poverty and improve peoples' livelihood, and agree to strengthen Africa and India cooperation in this sector in order to improve the food security of Africa and to increase its exports to world markets." The framework envisaged cooperation in, among other things, capacity building and sharing of experience in policy analysis and planning relating to the agriculture sector; cooperation in water resource management and irrigation practices, agro-infrastructure development, transfer of applied agricultural technology and skills transfer; and cooperation to combat agro-based diseases.

In recent years, particularly after the first India–Africa Summit, cooperation in the agriculture sector has intensified with East African countries. The Indian private sector has been investing in the agriculture sector. Many business enterprises such as Jain Irrigation, Karuturi Global Ltd. (KGL), Kirloskar Brothers Ltd. (KBL), Mahindra and Mahindra (M&M), Ruchi Soya and Renuka Sugars have established their presence in East African countries in agriculture and related sectors. In fact, Kirloskar Brothers has had a presence ever since the export of sugarcane cutters to Kenya as early as 1936. They have been providing adaptable, appropriate and affordable pumping systems and solutions to help address the need for irrigation in many countries across East Africa to help them develop their agricultural sector and achieve food security. In addition, several new players such as Yes Bank and McLeod Russel are making forays into the agriculture sector in the region.

The primary focus of the privates sector engagement in East Africa agriculture sector has been on four fundamental pillars: technologies, infrastructure, institutions and policies. It is felt that Indian investment in the agricultural sector of East Africa to become successful, must simultaneously address the interlocking issues of technology, infrastructure, institutions and policies. In this regard, the lessons learned from India's green revolution experiment of the 1960s and 1970s could be instructive[18]. Besides promoting research in agriculture is another area where both sides are working together. Indian scientific and agricultural research institutions have assisted around 5,000 entrepreneurs for developing their business ideas in the East African countries.

Despite the opportunities in the agriculture sector, it is observed that for investments, financing remains one of the crucial issues. Although financing is available across the agricultural value chain from land asset creation to agricultural inputs and even for processing and distribution, which is made available mostly through long term loans, yet it is in nascent stage and is not   enough to provide support to investors that is needed. Support is required to promote investments and encourage Indian investors in East Africa. EXIM bank, which is owned by the Government of India provides the necessary financial assistance to exporters and importers and coordinates between the institutions engaged with export and import to promote investments. It extends lines of credit (LOCs) as well, at concessional rates to East African countries. There are risks as well such as operational, social or political and therefore systems for risk mitigation need to be set in place.

Fisheries

There is a potential for development of various types of fish, shrimps, lobsters, seaweed and other marine resources in East Africa countries like Tanzania and Kenya, which Indian private sector can explore. Investors have freedom to choose suitable areas for: (i) Deep sea fishing; (ii) Fish Farming; and Processing and Canning.

Tanzania is endowed with some of the largest freshwater lakes in the world, occupying 53,480 sq. km (6 percent of the country's land mass), with substantial fish resources of 730,000 metric tons per year. Investment in fishing is regulated by the Fisheries Act of 1970 under the Ministry of Natural Resources and Tourism, which is responsible for licensing and quota allocation to guard against over-exploitation and environmental damage. Principal markets include the European Union and Japan for the Nile perch from Lake Victoria. Tanzania controls 55 percent of Lake Victoria but lags behind Kenya in fish-processing and export.

Health

There is a growing relationship emerging between private healthcare providers in India and East Africa, with India being now more proactive in supporting health initiatives in African countries. Under the year 2008 and 2011 India Africa Summit framework of cooperation various initiatives have been taken to strengthen cooperation with African countries in the health sectors. The private sector health care providers are increasingly playing greater role. India is emerging as a global health care provider because of its ability to offer world-class expertise at developing world costs. There has been a proliferation of new health care facilities at private centres of medical excellence in India. High-class medical infrastructure facilities, coupled with improved and cheaper air connections and easy access to visa facilities, are some of the factors that have contributed to the emerging scenario. An understanding of the public and Private Health care system in East African countries would provide an insight on the needs and requirements of basic health care where India, particularly its private sector can play an important role.

Private and public health provision in Tanzania and Kenya

The two East African countries of Kenya and Tanzania have a population of 37.5 million and 40.4 million respectively[19]. Health care facilities are structured in a pyramid model with government-run dispensaries forming the base level of the medical system primarily catering to simple ailments. Above that there are health centers, sub-district hospitals and provincial hospitals, which are referral points at district level. The more critical cases are sent to the national hospitals. Besides this his formal medical system there is a substantial system of 'traditional' health care.

Health care system in Kenya and Tanzania emphasizes on primary health care at affordable rates, making them pioneers in sub-Saharan Africa. As 70 per cent of the population in these countries lives in rural areas, more focus is given to the rural areas. Earlier the establishment of health facilities has taken into consideration facility/population ratio which over the period of time has been seriously overtaken in some areas by the high population growth rate. Moreover, good medical care is not within the reach of the majority the governments with considerable budgetary constraints have been the principal providers of both preventive and curative treatment. Moreover in the East African countries, the level of health financing is still insufficient to ensure equitable access to basic and essential health services and interventions, making adequacy and equity of resource mobilisation and allocation for health important. Fundamental to equitable health financing is the principle of financial protection, that no one in need of health services should be denied access due to inability to pay and that households' livelihoods should not be threatened by the costs of health care.[20] National policies pay some attention to these issues.

In Kenya, under Vision 2030 government pledges to provide resources to those who are excluded from health care by financial reasons. It further aims to implement a financing plan that involves the government, donors and other stakeholders. In Tanzania, the Poverty Reduction Strategy Paper provides for financing of poverty alleviation efforts including primary health care and water while policies for specific areas (AIDS, elderly) include provisions to mobilize resources for services for these vulnerable groups, including protection against inability to pay. In Uganda, the National Health Policy (NHP) recognizes the role of public expenditure in protecting the most vulnerable population. It provides that the government should continue to allocate and spend an increasing proportion of its annual health budget (both domestic and external resources) to provide a minimum health care package in the medium term. However the resources are not enough.[21] There is a wide chasm between needs and the resource pool, which has worsened in the wake of the current credit crunch. In fact the healthcare system in the East African countries was hit hard by the 'structural adjustment' policies introduced and imposed by the International Monetary Fund and the World Bank in the 1980s. Their insistence on low inflation rates and cuts in wage and budgetary expenditure in borrowing countries have proved detrimental to social sectors like health, with particularly damaging impacts for the poor.

Besides the resource crunch, from the people's pout of view the public health delivery in East Africa is not affordable, accessible and is of value. The health infrastructure is very poor marred by limited capability in terms of its human resource and in numbers of staff as compared to the level of pressing health issues, including the HIV/AIDS and other diseases. Moreover the personnel shortage is compounded with the flow of health professionals to other resourceful countries in search of better employment opportunities. Public provision is also mired with problems of poor management and corruption. Hospitals often work under highly unfavourable conditions, especially the public hospitals which lack the basic infrastructure for healthcare. There is little access to healthcare because the poor, who form a sizeable section of the population, are unable to pay either the user fees or the transport costs.[22]

The problem is compounded by the fact that the continent is heavily dependent on imported pharmaceutical products that lead to the high cost of medicine. The vagaries of transportation at times results in the withdrawal of medicines, including life-saving drugs, from the market. Traditional healers and birth attendants continue to be important providers of health services, especially in rural areas and poorer urban areas, such as Kibera in Nairobi.[23]

According to the World Bank sources and based on household budget surveys, 36 per cent of the population of Tanzania lives below the national poverty line, and life expectancy at birth in Tanzania is only 52 years[24]. Total government expenditure on health as a percentage of gross domestic products in 2006 was 6.4 per cent whereas private expenditure on health as percentage of total expenditure on health in the same year was 42.2 per cent. External resources as a percentage of total expenditure on health comprised 27.8 per cent in 2006. In the following year the total government expenditure on health as a percentage of gross domestic products fell to 5.3 per cent while the corresponding data for external resources as a percentage of total expenditure on health rose to 49.9 per cent[25].

Tanzania

Following independence, healthcare was considered to be the domain of the state, with limited number of private health facilities provided in major towns of the country. In 1977 there was a ban on 'private health service for profit' as an outcome of the nationalization of all the hospitals including those run by the Christian Missions in 1975. It was believed by the leaders then human health should not be commoditized. This, however, impacted negatively on the delivery of health services, as it led to the roll back of the private sector and resulted in the shrinking of the supply of medical services[26]. Later after about a decade and a half the government recognized the role of the private sector in healthcare with the law being amended with the Private Hospitals (Regulation) Amendment Act 1991, whereby qualified medical practitioners and dentists could run private hospitals with the permission of the Ministry of Health.

Given the fact that the health infrastructure is weak, the phenomenon of medical tourism from Tanzania has taken strides. More affluent patients have been going abroad for treatment or have been treated by foreign doctors since the early 1980s. Efforts have been made to get treatment for Tanzanians in India as well. Since 1986, many children have been sent to Mumbai through the sponsorship of the Lions Club, Dar-es-Salaam and the Ministry of Health in Tanzania. Over the past few years, about 1,000 Tanzanian patients have sought treatment at the Apollo Hospital in Hyderabad, the Madras Medical Mission in Chennai, and the Narayan Hrudalaya Heart Institute in Bangalore, under the guidance of the internationally reputed heart surgeons, with discounted fees, which include boarding and lodging.

The former president of India, Dr Abdul Kalam, in his capacity as patron of the Care Hospital in Hyderabad, donated ten free heart surgeries for Tanzanian patients. He also offered cardiac surgery training for government doctors, who were to be identified through the Tanzania Ministry of Health at the same hospital. Over the past three decades about 2,000 heart surgeries have been facilitated in Indian hospitals because of the international quality medical standards and near 100 per cent success rate (about 99 per cent) at one-third the cost of similar surgery in developed nations. Tanzanians have also been sent to Manipal hospital in the state of Karnataka, for treatment of kidney ailments and dialysis, given the lack of a kidney treatment centre in their country. Although India is able to provide relatively affordable medical treatment, this is still something only affluent Africans can afford, leaving the vast majority of the population under-served. In Tanzania every year more than 7,000 children with congenital heart disease and adolescents with rheumatic heart diseases await open-heart surgery treatment.

Efforts have been made by doctors to get financial assistance through various international communities and charities in order to import state-of-the-art medical and surgical facilities that are unavailable in Tanzania. However, these would still be within the private sector and thus inaccessible to the poor.

Treatment in private Tanzanian hospitals such as Aga Khan Hospital is expensive and patients often have no choice as these are the better equipped hospitals. The other hospitals, which are run by cultural associations and donations from Indian trust are somewhat relatively cheaper, but still unaffordable for many patients.

Sometimes Indian doctors visit Tanzania and patients are informed about the visits ahead of time and the dates and venues of their consultations are advertised on the Indian television channels in Dar-es-Salaam and in local newspapers. Those diagnosed with complicated aliments they are advised by the visiting Indian doctor to travel to India for advance treatment. Such tie ups with Indian Private hospitals sometimes fill the gap of limited technically trained doctors in Tanzania, however it only benefits a few people

Kenya

In Kenya also the medical health care facilities is critical, with limited trained doctors, nurses to run hospitals, and constrained funding. In the period between 2000 and 2002 the government was scheduled to lay off 5,300 health staff, as a consequence of conditionalities imposed by the International Monetary Fund (IMF) and World Bank in the 1980s as a part of their structural adjustment programme. This had a severe impact on the local health clinics and dispensaries as they had fewer supplies and medicines. Medicals standards deteriorated in the public hospitals. Even many trained doctors and nurses have moved to South Africa, Botswana, Lesotho and Swaziland for better packages. Treatments in private hospitals are very high. Those who can mobilize resources opt to travel to countries like India for treatment.

Currently, however, Kenya has committed to spending 15 percent of its national budget on healthcare amid plans to transform itself into a middle income nation by 2030. With public-private partnerships (PPPs) shaping the healthcare market and membership of the EAC trading bloc reducing regulatory hurdles to entry, Kenya is forecast to have a CAGR of 17 percent through 2016. This reflects opportunities in both communicable diseases, such as malaria and HIV, and NCDs which are a growing challenge in the country. There are opportunities for investments by Indian private sectors in the health sector in Kenya to provide access to affordable health care. For the countries of East Africa India has become destination for medical tourism.

India as a destination for medical tourism

East African patients can access quality treatment at Indian hospitals. The Indian diaspora, particularly the Gujaratis in East Africa, who have roots and established connections on both sides of the Indian Ocean, have come to India for treatment.

There is no organised manner of referrals for potential patients who seek treatment in India. The initial contact with Indian doctors is established through referrals by their local consultants or through initial contact with Indian medical practitioners who visit East Africa through local religious, philanthropic organisations such as the Lions or Rotary International or through private hospitals.[27]

Through various associations and general practitioners, doctors in India also approach prospective patients in east African countries. There are also hospitals who regularly send their teams to Tanzania and Kenya to set up initial contact with patients through various medical centres in Tanzania and Kenya. Promotional tours are also conducted by Indian hospitals. For instance to promote Apollo as a destination for healthcare, representatives was sent to the ITB Exhibition of travel and tourism held in Berlin in 2003. The response was overwhelming and Apollo has started an inter-national marketing division thereafter.[28] The attraction of India is because of cheaper healthcare because of the rupee value. Besides, there are medical tourism facilitators, such as AAREX India, Fire Runner Healthcare Consultants, Infotrex Services Private Limited and Medical tourism in Gujarat.com, who get in touch with patients in East African countries through the internet and link them to Indian hospitals according to the nature of treatment required, the budget and other preferences.[29] However, some of these agencies are criticized for corruption.

Pharmaceutical

Indian pharmaceutical industry has attained a unique position in the world market including East Africa. Indian pharmaceutical companies are fast becoming multinational firms with production facilities across various continents. 14 percent of India's $8 billion pharmaceutical exports in 2009 went to East Africa, the role it has played in controlling the spread of HIV/AIDS and other diseases by making treatment affordable cannot be ignored. Indian pharmaceutical companies have been a natural extension of domestic market because of similar pattern of tropical diseases. The Indian companies have not only been exporting pharmaceutical products for last several years to Africa but also have set up pharmaceutical plants under joint ventures. For East Africa, Indian pharmaceutical industry is a source to acquire generic medicines. With the technical capability and price competitiveness Indian Pharmaceutical companies have a long way to go in East Africa.

Kenya, Tanzania and Uganda provide a major market for India's pharmaceutical industry – Besides pharma companies like Ranbaxy are not just selling to these countries but have set up production facilities there. Moreover, in an instance of very pertinent technology transfer, Cipla decided in May 2008 to jumpstart the local manufacture of key antiretroviral drugs to combat HIV/AIDS as a result of which the Ugandan local partner will be producing these drugs with Indian technology at a cost that can be as low as $10. Apart from the fact that HIV/AIDS is endemic in all the countries of the region, local production will also generate employment to trained scientists and mid-level pharmaceutical workers in a country where unemployment runs at around 35 percent. [30]

The rate of growth of export in the recent years, have overtaken the rate of growth of domestic pharmaceutical industry. Export of pharmaceuticals to East Africa is growing with the time. In fact East Africa as a market for pharmaceutical product is growing faster than other overseas market.

The reason for India's surging export in pharmaceutical is attributed to following reasons. The cost of manufacturing drugs in India is still comparatively cheaper in India as a result it can compete in the global market. It is for cheaper rate of production, Indian companies get better profit margin in the international market, including East Africa. The export increases the market base of the Indian companies, which further add to profit margin and plant efficiency. There is cheaper bank finance available for export from several Indian banks, which removes problem of finance significantly. Two additional domestic problems, drug price control and excise and sales tax does not apply on exports. It is a great advantage for the Indian firm as they further add to profit. Finally, over the years the Indian generic medicine has created international market reputation for itself, as a result extra efforts to push products are not required. Indian pharmaceutical products are easily accepted in East Africa.

East African markets accounts for up to 20 percent of India's annual drug exports of Rs 39,500 crores[31]. It is the largest supplier of pharmaceuticals and chemicals to Uganda (30 percent of its imports); in 2007-08, Kenya imported Rs. 342.4 crores worth of medicines; Ranbaxy alone sold medicines worth Rs. 563 crores in Africa in 2008. However, in December 2008, the Anti-Counterfeit Act was brought before the Kenyan parliament, which recognises intellectual property rights registered in any country of the world. This implies that even if a drug is not patented in Kenya (where it is sold) or in India (where it is manufactured) but in a third country, it would still be considered as counterfeit in Kenya. This would obviously harm India's pharmaceuticals sale, and India's concern was that other East African countries like Uganda and Tanzania may soon follow Kenya. According to the Indian Pharmaceuticals Alliance (IPA), this is part of a smear campaign by Western multinationals unable to cope with the competition provided by India's cheap and efficient medicines. Developed countries had earlier failed to get a regime implemented through the World Intellectual Property Organisation (WIPO) that would make a patent granted in one country applicable worldwide. [32]

However, what is more significant for India vis a vis East African states is that a majority of them are on the other side of the table in the ongoing talks to review the World Health Organisation's (WHO) definition of 'counterfeiting'. While India opposes all attempts to link intellectual property issues with 'counterfeiting', African countries appear to feel otherwise.

The Kenyan definition is contrary to the IP Act, 2001, and does not distinguish between different categories of goods (for example, counterfeit trade mark goods, printed copyright products) as is one in WTO's Trade Related Aspects of Intellectual Property Rights (TRIPS) regime. Since these are issues that have the potential to sour relations attempts have been made to get it resolved through diplomatic negotiations at the local, bilateral and international levels.

Government level efforts are being made and besides that, to mitigate misconceptions that generic drugs from India are counterfeit and/or spurious, domestic pharma lobby groups the Indian Pharmaceutical Alliance (IPA) and Indian Drug Manufacturers Association, as well as individual companies, are launching programmes to educate patients and non-governmental organizations (NGOs) in those countries about the effect of such laws on access to affordable essential medicines. A plan of action for an awareness campaign among users of generic drugs in East African countries is also in progress by the government.

To access market and to establish clients, the export professionals employ a mix strategy. The country visit is compulsory as indicated by professionals. All of them visit East Africa, on a regular basis to study the prospects of their products and to locate actual buyer. They prefer establishing products in a country before shifting to other countries. The product they sale in Africa are generally their established products in the domestic Indian market. In order to access market, a lot of help is sought through Indian professional contacts. Exchange of information and views among fellow professionals is commonly observed. The information are based on firsthand experience and thus are authentic. The information about the nature of a particular country, prospects for products and the information about the local buyer are sought from fellow professional before entering into final negotiation.

The help of export promotion council, chamber of commerce are of no significant help to access market. The Pharmaceutical Export Promotion Council (PHARMEXCIL) is a dedicated export promotion council of the government of India. However professional do not find it very effective in terms of market access. Similarly, other chambers of commerce are also not commonly of support to access African Market including East Africa. Professionals prefer exhibition and buyer seller meet as a tool to access market, however they are not frequently organised. Professionals emphasize the need to have more such events. Finally, Internet is the least preferred way to access market.

Indian pharmaceutical exporters prefer two methods of doing business in Africa, through its own established offices and through a local partner/ buyer. However, the latter option generally preferred as it offers advantages. The cost of establishing office is higher and unless substantial volume of business is regularly done, establishing office becomes unviable. The local partner takes care of liaisoning with local authorities like customs and drug controlling authorities efficiently.

The customs and drug controlling authorities, both in India as well in the East African countries are important factor in export. The professionals indicated that they faced no major problem with either of customs or drug controlling authorities. However, the concerns about the increasingly stringent regulations adopted by the East African drug authorities were raised. The registration of drug is also getting costlier over the period of time.

In the financial transactions, letter of credit is preferred mode of transaction. Cash in advance is too sought in East Africa however credit and loans are negligible in East Africa. Professionals repel popular notion that doing business in East Africa is risky, however they suggest necessary precaution. The most important precaution professionals observe is that the letters of credit are issued from the banks from United States or from countries of European origin. They generally do not prefer letter of credit from African or Indian bank. In the case when letter of credit is extended through African banks, they prefer to endorse it by Banks from United States or Europe.

The interaction with the Indian governmental is mixed. The interaction with PHARMEXCIL is rated low to medium. It is not as supportive in market related information, access or as a group of collective bargain. The Export Import Bank of India (EXIM Bank) is second vital organization. However professional have low interaction with the bank. Similarly, the Export Credit Guarantee Corporation of India (ECGC) has low interaction among pharmaceutical exporters. The ECGC policies are seen as extra cost to the export which directly affects the profit margin. However, need base policy are sought from the ECGC to mitigate risk. The interaction with Indian Embassies/High commissions too is rated low. There appears to be division among approach to the governmental agencies. The bigger export establishment interacts with higher frequency whereas small and medium enterprises are not so forthcoming.

About competitors for Indian pharmaceutical countries the views are varied. Competition are seen from China, South East Asian countries and multinational companies. However, it is observed that, Indian companies are the biggest competitors for other Indian companies in East Africa.

The Indian pharmaceutical sector is well placed to compete. It has achieved technical capability and has large pool of technically qualified manpower. Above all, the cost of production is much cheaper in India in comparison to its competitors. It is for above mentioned factors that East African nations have been attracted towards Indian companies. However, it is far short of desired level as including East African countries continues to suffer from falling health profile and would require more and more affordable medicines. The Indian pharmaceutical industry has a long way to go in East Africa.

Besides exports of pharmaceuticals products, Indian private players in field of medicine are now setting up local manufacturing capacities to make the East African countries self-sufficient in cheap and quality drugs. Since these markets are short of raw materials, Indian companies are benefitting from exporting active pharma ingredients. Cipla, India's largest generics manufacturer by sales, helped commission a plant under the local management of Quality Chemicals Industries Ltd (QCIL) in Uganda in the year 2009. The project is a joint venture between QCIL and the Ugandan government, with technology inputs from Cipla. Other companies like Ranbaxy, and Dr Reddy are also venturing into manufacturing.

East African countries offer good opportunities for Indian private players in medicine, for which over the years Indian pharmaceutical companies have increased their presence in these countries, despite the challenges relating to regulatory mechanisms and counterfeit proposal by EAC.

Information Technology and Enabled Services

India has a vibrant private ICT sector which primarily drives the IT sector, well supported by the Government. Countries in East Africa, such as Kenya, Tanzania and Uganda on the other hand have a strong government support for ICT development and adoption. Inspired by the successes of India's IT and telecom sector, East African countries have embarked on a road to develop their own information technology (IT)-enabled services sector in contact centers, financial sectors, manufacturing, business process outsourcing, and software development. Indian top private software services companies like TCS, Infosys, Wipro have ventured into these countries to seize the abundant opportunities by investing in key areas such as Information and Communication Technology (ICT) development. They are eager to win customers and market share in the region that is home to fast-growing enterprises and under-developed technology infrastructure. They are fast expanding their employee base and delivery centres in a market that was earlier viewed as a low-cost, near-shore delivery location to serve large outsourcing customers in Europe and West Asia.[33] Primarily IT services growth in the East African region is being strongly driven by government spends in IT infrastructure and services.[34]

Indian software, enjoy a substantial uptake in the local banking sector. It is currently being used by Kenya Commercial Bank, the Equity bank and Orange Money to drive mobile banking services. *Manam Infotech*, another Indian company, is also providing software services to *Mobibank*, part of the Kenya Commercial Bank, said to have the biggest branch network in East Africa. *Manam's* software currently allows *Mobibank's* customers to access a range of banking services from their handsets. Indian software companies are also making an impact away from the financial services sector. *RMSI*, a specialist in geographic information systems (GIS), for instance, is said to be working on a process to digitise Kenya's land registry, considerably easing any search for title deeds. Other IT projects have also been undertaken by a number of other Indian suppliers, notably Mahindra Saytam, Infosys and Tata.[35]

Besides the software services, in the telecommunication sector India has made significant inroads. In late March 2010, Bharti Airtel, a New Delhi based corporate telecommunications giants, announced the successful completion of a multi-billion dollar deal that has led to taking control of the African operations of Kuwaiti firm Zain in some 13 countries including East Africa. The success of the deal, after repeated failures of both Bharti and Reliance Industries merger with South Africa's MTN since 2008, in a way heralded the potential of Indian telecom firms to diversify in Africa's telecom sector. The absolute scale of the deal (reported to be worth $10.7 billion) briefly captured the limelight not only Indian media but also those of Africa, and the business sections of western newspapers.

Bharti Airtel is now second largest mobile service provider, in East Africa while another Indian company, Essar, occupies the fourth place. The headquarters of Bharti's East African operations are located in Nairobi, a convenient investment hub and a gateway to the eastern African region. Bharti flying its colours in Kenya's capital was not the first such act by an Indian firm. In 2008 Essar, another major Indian conglomerate, inaugurated Kenya's' fourth mobile phone network after a $500 million injection the previous year. In July 2009, Essar also acquired a 50 per cent share in Kenya Petroleum Refineries, the sole oil refinery in eastern Africa.[36]

East Africa is also serviced by the Indian Pan-African e-network, an ambitious IT initiative between India and the African Union first mooted in 2004. The project was designed to connect the 53 AU member states through satellite and fibre optic network to India and to each other. This is in order to enable access to and the sharing of expertise between India and the African nations in the areas of tele-education, telemedicine, voice over Internet protocols, infotainment, resource mapping, meteorological services, e-government and e-commerce. It is one of the successful projects that has enabled the East African countries to bridge digital divide and strengthen connectivity. It is giving East Africa-India relations a new substance and content. It is not only bridging the digital divide, it is bridging the divide between the have and the have-nots."

Kenya, Uganda and Tanzania have been the early beneficiaries of this project. 'The e- network links up regional universities, learning centres, super specialty hospitals and remote hospitals from east African countries with six universities and five super specialty hospitals from .The e-network project however has several opportunities and challenges. The project is indeed novel and people-oriented, but its success will depend on its effective implementation.[37] The ultimate test of the project lies in shaping this government-to-government model into a sustainable model of private-public partnership which is cost-effective and affordable for the common man.

East Africa has the opportunity to use the services of Indian technical experts and Indian private software companies to improve their ICT connectivity and extend it to the remote areas.

Infrastructure Development in East Africa

As we have seen that East African economies are not only growing but also becoming more favourable environments for businesses and investors. Investing in East Africa has the potential both to generate returns and to create beneficial long-term relationships. One of the most promising areas for investing in East Africa's boom is infrastructure.

Improved infrastructure will set the stage for further growth on the continent, creating large markets and investment opportunities. According to the World Bank, addressing East Africa's infrastructure gap could add two percentage points to its rate of GDP growth. [38]

East Africa's growth is already creating new business opportunities in the infrastructure sector or private companies, infrastructure will be worth US$ 200 billion in annual revenue by 2020. [39]

Returns on foreign investment in East African infrastructure are higher than in any other developing region. East African governments are increasingly recognizing the importance of the private sector for the provision of infrastructure. Many have made serious efforts to create the right legislative, regulatory and institutional environment for private investors to come on board.

Indian private sector players are increasingly positioning themselves to capitalise on East African infrastructure opportunities. Unlike China, infrastructure-related investments have played only an auxiliary role in India's thrust into Africa. Given India's own infrastructure-deficit, it is no surprise that India's infrastructure-related firms are underweight in East Africa. It is certainly worth stressing that India plans to spend US$1.5 trillion (tr) by 2015 to overhaul its own creaky infrastructure. Nevertheless, clear structural synergies are materializing.[40]

In recent years, Indian financing and technical assistance for East African infrastructure has displayed meaningful gains. The majority of Indian financing for projects in Africa is channeled through the India Exim Bank, which extends lines of credit (LOCs) to African governments or regional institutions, many of which are intended for direct infrastructure projects. Half of Indian LoCs to Africa have a direct infrastructure focus. While the majority of the LOCs fall within the $10 mn to $50 mn range, sizeable commitments to East African countries and Development (EBID) act as an indication of the strategic significance of support for the Indian government, particularly in East African countries rich in natural resources.

Though in the case of infrastructure development, India has historically played a key role in East Africa's physical infrastructure development, yet for the benefits of the engagements to reach a larger number of countries, and also for Indian engagement to upscale, there is need for a higher level of regional coordination in east Africa. It has been said that projects like laying fibre optic cables, building roads and power transmission lines are taken up across countries, and the economies of scale would benefit an entire region.

Rwanda has invited India to participate in the economic development of the East African nation through investment in the infrastructure along with other sectors. The country has been trying to attract foreign investment in infrastructure, especially roads, airports and real estate.

L&T secured two large World Bank-financed turnkey contracts worth $100 mn. The Songo Songo Gas Development and Power Generation Project involves collecting gas from three offshore and two onshore wells, processing it in the gas plant and piping it 215 km to Dar es Salaam. It is also constructing a pure soda ash plant for Magadi Soda Company Ltd in Kenya.

Conclusion

The economic landscape of the East Africa region in the last decade has maintained healthy and sustained annual growth. This sub-region has earned its place not only as the most rapidly growing region in sub-Saharan Africa but also in the developing world through extensive macroeconomic stabilization and policy reforms. Since 2005, the east African countries have annual average Gross Domestic Product (GDP) growth rates of close to 8 per cent. The region has proved its resilience by weathering global shocks, including the 2008-09 surges in international fuel and food prices. It is emerging as a significant investment destination. This is because it has a stable political environment, and reasonable level of governance and democracy and a market access to over 130 million people with combined Gross Domestic Product (GDP) of about US$ 75 billion. Moreover business friendly reforms have led to drawing foreign direct investments to the region. The region offers immense opportunities to Indian private sector for trade and investment.

Indian investments in the agriculture sector are not only improving farm technologies and productivity in East Africa. They are also promoting agro-business through technical assistance and skills transfers. This is an area with good scope for Indian companies. In the health sector, Indian pharmaceutical companies have established a large presence in the East African countries by providing them with wide range of quality and affordable generic drugs. Government budgetary allocations to the public health sectors is witnessing a constant increase. Indian companies like Airtel has revolutionized East Africa's telecom sector. The regional growth in ICT is driven by consumer demand, public and private sector demand and government support. With a growing market the region offers many opportunities for Indian industry.

The EAC potentially provides a great opportunity to connect up with the COMESA and the SADC as mentioned earlier, and to the African hinterland particularly because these countries re-exports much of its imports to other African countries thus virtually providing an opening to many other countries. As such, it is important for India to cooperate both bilaterally with the individual states and with the EAC. India's trade and investment have been growing steadily with all three countries of the region in the sectors such as agriculture, pharmaceuticals, ICT and infrastructure.

Although China's investment presence in East Africa is more widely seen, and China's stronger political cohesion and economic heft can bring more FDI projects on board, there is room for Indian private sectors, between the Western and Chinese investors pouring into Africa. Local leaders often decry China's investment and development strategy as resembling the exploitative, extractive methods of former colonial powers. India's broader portfolio investments guided by a historical connection to a greater Indian Ocean community, conversely, are an alternative to the Chinese approach.

Indian private sector has contributed in strengthening the relations, which are preceded by much deeper economic, political and cultural connections between India and East Africa. Not surprisingly then, perceptions of contemporary relations between India and countries of East Africa have been inflected by this heritage of connectivity. Indian investors are becoming increasingly prominent in the East African countries. . .

End Notes

1   Bhattacharya, Sanjukta ,'Engaging Africa: India's interest in the African continent, past and present', in Cheru, F. and Obi, C. (eds) The Riseof China and India in Africa, London and Uppsala, Zed Books and The Nordic Africa Institute, 2010

2   Mawdsley Emma and McCann, Gerard, 'The elephant in the corner? Reviewing India-Africa relations in the new millennium', Geography Compass, vol. 4, no. 2, pp. 81-93, 2010

3   Rao S.R, Exim Bank: partnership in Africa's development', presentation made at the Organisation for Economic Cooperation and Development (OECD), Paris, 16-17 March, 2000

4   Rao S.R.'Exim Bank: partnership in Africa's development', presentation made at the Organisation for Economic Cooperation and Development (OECD), Paris, 16-17 March,2006

5   Goldstein A. et al The Rise of China and India: What's in it for Africa? Paris: OECD. 2006

6   Rao S.R. 'Exim Bank: partnership in Africa's development', presentation made at the Organisation for Economic Cooperation and Development (OECD), Paris, 16-17 March, 2006

7   CII 5th Conclave on India Africa Project Partnership 2009, Celebrating Partnerships, 22nd -24th March 2009, New Delhi, India

8   Suresh Kumar, A perspective on Indian trade and investments in East Africa, India–Africa, December 1, 2010, "http://www.africa india org/ index. php? option=com_content&view=article&id=51:aperspective-on-indian-trade-and-investments-in-east-africa&catid=34:agriculture-sector&Itemid=29"http:// www.africaindia.org/indexphp?option=com_content&view=article&id=51:a-

perspective-on-indian-trade-and-investments-in-east-africa&catid=
34:agriculture-sector&Itemid=29

9   On the Ground, Africa-India trade and investment – Playing to strengths,
     Standard Chartered Bank, Global Research, 08 August 2012

10   Suresh Kumar, no 8

11   ibid

12   Speaking at a half-day seminar (1st March, 2013) on "Doing business with
     India" in Dar- es- Salaam, the Export Processing Zones Authority (EPZA)
     Director General Dr Adelhelm Meru and Tanzania Investment Centre (TIC)
     Executive Director Raymond Mbilinyi, described the country as the best
     investment destination in the region with immense business opportunities
     and political stability.

13   Asia News Agency Pvt Ltd, http://teleradproviders.com/nbn/print.php?id=
     MjcONzE=&page=c3Rvcnk=

14   India–Africa Connect, India Pledges &191 for Tanzania to jointly combat piracy,
     "http://www.indiaafricaconnect.in/index.php?param=news/2655scaling-
     a-new-summit/123" http://www.indiaafricaconnect.in/index.php? param=
     news/2655/scaling-a-new-summit/123

15   Boosting ties: India offers millions but Tanzania wants more, India Today,
     Dar-es- Salaam, May 28, 2011 "http://indiatoday.intoday.in/story/india-offers-
     millions-but-tanzania-wants-more-grants/1/139601.html" \t"_blank_"http://
     indiatoday.intoday.in/story/india-offers-millions-but-tanzania-wants-more-
     grants/1/139601.html)

16   Report on South South Cooperation Induia, Africa and Food Security: Between
     the Summits, http://www.mu.ac.in/arts/social_scienceafrican_studiesConference
     percent20Report, percent20SSC- percent20India, percent20Africa percent20and
     percent2Food percent20Security percent20January percent202011.pdf

17   ibid

18   ibid

19   World Bank, 'Kenya at a glance', 24 September 2009, http://devdata.worldbank.
     org/AAG/ken_aag.pdf,"http://devdata.worldbank.org/AAG/ken_aag.pdf,
     accessed 16 March 2009

20   Makrere University,A review of Kenyan, Ugandan and Tanzanian public health law relevant to equity in health t http://www.cehurd.org/wp-content/uploads/2011/01/Review-of-Public-Health-Laws-and-Policies-in-Kenya-Uganda-and-Tanzania.pdf

21   ibid

22   Renu Modi, Offshore healthcare management: medical tourism between Kenya, Tanzania and India, http://www.indoafricanbusiness.com/healthcare.php, accessed on 20 November 2013

23   ibid

24   World Bank, 'Tanzania at a glance', 24 September, http://devdata.worldbank.org/AAG/tza_aag.pdf,"http://devdata.worldbank.org/AAG/tza_aag.pdf, 2008,accessed 16 March 2009

25   World Health Organisation, 'Health expenditure', in World Health Statistics, "http://www.who.int/whosis/whostat/EN_WHS10_Part2.pdf,"http://www.who.int/whosis/whostat/EN_WHS10_Part2.pdf, 2010,accessed 10 October 2010

26   Government of Tanzania, 'Hotuba ya Waziri wa Afya Mheshimiwa Anna Margareth Abdallah, Mbunge, kuhusu Makadirio ya Matumizi ya Fedha kwa Mwaka', "http://www.tanzania.go.tz/health.html,"http://www.tanzania.go.tz/health.html, 2002/03, accessed 12 April 2010.

27   No.22

28   Medindia, 'India emerging as international medical tourism hub', "http://www.medindia.net/news/healthwatch/India-"http://www.medindia.net/news/healthwatch/India-   Emerging-as-International-Medical-Tour,   22 September, 2008 ,accessed 11 November 2009

29   No 22

30   http://www.thaidian.com/newsportal/health/technology-from-india-makes-aids-drugs-in-uganda_10053777.html, accessed on May2, 2012.)

31   Live Mint, Wall Street Journal, 16 February 2010, http://www.livemint.com/Companies/mMIRJi9gnndoxpUd3KOqhK/Indian-drug-makers-worried-by-East-Africa8217s-legal-prop.html, accessed on 30 November 2013

32   Economic Times, New Delhi, May 2, 2009

33   IT Voice, Why Indian IT companies like TCS, Infosys and Wipro are investing in Africa, May 10, 2014, http://www.itvoice.in/index.php/it-voice-news/why-indian-it-companies-like-tcs-infosys-and-wipro-are-investing-in-africa, Accessed on 1 June 2014

34   ibid

35   Research, 17 July 2013,China and India compete for market share in East Africa,   http://economists-pick-research.hktdc.com/business-news/article/ International-Market-News/China-and-India-compete-for-market-share-in-East-African-economies/imn/en/1/1X0, accessed on 30 November 2013

36   ibid

37   Sanjukta Bhattacharya, India East Africa Ties, Africa Quarterly, Vol 49, No 1, Feb-April 2009,

38   Briceno-Garmendia C and Foster V (2010) 'Africa's Infrastructure –A Time for Transformation

39   McKinsey Global Institute (2010) 'Lions on the move – the progress and potential of African Economies'

40   Simon Freemantle, Indian Construction Firms making inroads into Africa,5 November 2010, http://www.howwemadeitinafrica.com/indian-construction-firms-making-inroads-into-africa/4794/, Accessed on 2 December 2014

Chapter - 4

Indian Diaspora in East Africa as Heritage Resource

Introduction

The diaspora is one of the contemporary global forces shaping the directions and trends of international development in the 21st century. Increasingly developing country governments are focusing and trying to engage with their Diaspora resources. There is increasing awareness among the developing countries of their "Diasporas" and their potential for development and economic growth. Today they are considered a key strategic asset since they are social, financial, intellectual & political capitals having the potential to contribute to their home country's development.

In fact, in recent years, the potential of a country's Diaspora resources in national development efforts and strengthening bilateral relations between the host and home countries, has gained growing international recognition, both in political and academic/research circles, as well as among diaspora members themselves. Increasingly, developing country governments, diaspora community organizations, and others in the development industry are asking: how can Diasporas be mobilized to transfer skills, knowledge, resources to contribute to the socioeconomic development of their countries of origin, build networks for promoting business and economic engagement and enhance bilateral relations? This chapter aims to examine Indian diaspora in East Africa as a heritage resource. The key question that it explores is whether this heritage resource has the potential to promote India's engagement with East African countries. The Chapter is divided into two sections. The first section attempts at understanding the Indian diaspora as a heritage resource by focusing on their historical settlement and linkages, their identity in terms of language, culture, religion, their positioning in their host countries taking into account their role, status, and minority experiences. Taking into consideration their potential and concerns, the second section analyses whether the Indian diaspora as a heritage resource in East Africa, can be strategically significant in enhancing bilateral relations.

Section I

Indian Diaspora in East Africa

Out of the 12 million People of Indian Origin (PIO) spread in 136 countries[1], 2.42 million Indians are in Africa and East Africa comprises of 204500 Indians (Kenya comprising about 100000, followed by Tanzania near about 90000 and then Uganda- 12,000, the lesser number owing to historical reasons). East Africa has been a favourite destination for Indian immigrants since centuries. The region assumes immense significance for Indians because of multiple reasons. First, a large number of Indians migrated to East Africa compared to any other area in Africa. It is a region that saw the worst kind of crisis of PIOs, which was in Uganda. It is also a region towards which Indians leaders before independence and latter on government of India actively engaged itself both for association and disassociation with PIOs. Known as *Muhindi* (or *Wahindi* in plural) among local population, Peoples of Indian Origin (PIOs) are economically most prosperous community in the region. Though they constitute less than 0.5 per cent of the total population of the region, but they control major chunk of economies of these countries.[2] They immigrated into different bursts and different capacities to the region.

Migration and Indian Settlement: An Overview

The Indians knew the Coast of East Africa since ancient times. The 'Vedas' and 'Shrimad Bhagwat Geeta', the ancient Indian epics provide valuable information regarding contacts between the two regions. Daniel D.C. Don Nanjira rightly says "If we consider all early invaders of East Africa to have been foreign visitors or traders, then Indians (Hindus) were definitely among the invaders whose connections with the East African coast go back many centuries before Christ."[3]

These connections got fresh inputs in mid 19th century with the establishment of British rule in India and emergence of British naval supremacy in the Indian Ocean. During 1840-60, the population of the Indian settlers in Zanzibar increased from 1000 to over 5000. The greatest increase was in the number of artisans. The dominant group were the trader's and all the Indians came to be referred to as 'Banyani' (from Bania, a pejorative term used for the Vaishyas, the third rank in the Hindu Varna system). The total capital invested by Indians in Zanzibar was placed at 1.6 million British Pounds in 1873, a huge sum for a small country of 100,000 people at that time.[4] The most successful businessmen were the Ismaili Khojas whose spiritual leader was the Aga Khan. Tara Topan was the most prominent of the Ismaili's. Among the other well-settled groups were the Bhattias (the most prominent of whom was Jairam Sewji, the customs collector in Zanzibar), the Lohans, the Vanias, the Bohras and the Memons.[5]

The partition of Africa after the Berlin conference in 1884 and the subsequent opening up to the interior of Africa under European administration had far reaching implications for the traditional Indian association with the coast. The Congo basin treaties signed in 1885 by thirteen European countries and the United States of America led to the regulation of territorial rights and commercial development in the whole of East and Central Africa. The extension of British administration in the eastern part of Africa enabled the Indians settled in Zanzibar to move to the mainland. The Royal charter of 1888 made specific mention of the fact that the possession of the mainland by the company 'would be advantageous to the commercial and other interests of our subjects in the Indian Ocean, who may otherwise become compelled to reside or trade under the government or under the protection of alien powers.' The company's activities also gained from the presence of Indian merchants and artisans-particularly at Mombasa. One of the Indian merchant in-fact owed his career in East Africa to a contract received from the company in 1890 to recruit Indian workers and police for service in the company's territories.[6]

During this period, settlement of Indian communities moved to the mainland of East Africa. By 1887 there were somewhat more Indians outside Zanzibar Island than there were in the Island. Business communities of India like Khojas, Bohras, Sindhis, Memans, Parsees etc.got involved not only in Zanzibar but also in the places like Mombas, Dar-es-Salam, Jumba. Till 1887 the population of Indian settlers in East Africa reached 6345, out of them 3086 were in Zanzibar only. Now Indian communities emerged as the most affluent and influential businessmen in the region. Table No. I show the region wise presence of different Indian communities in the East Africa in 1887.

Settlement of indenture Indian agriculturists, in East Africa was another supporting factor, during this period- particularly as it was felt that both the climate and the presence of the Indian commercial community would facilitate the task of the Indian agriculturists. The thinking of the time was best explained by Lugard:

"From the overcrowded provinces of India especially, colonists might be drawn, and this would effect a relief to congested districts. From them we could draw labourers, both artisans and coolies, while they might also afford a recruiting ground for soldiers and police. The wants, moreover, of these more civilized settlers would.... Very greatly add to the exports.... Moreover, the methods of agriculture.... Would soon be imitated by the African"[7]

Such considerations - that did not of course materialize-were not confined to the British sphere alone. German authorities, perhaps taking their cue from the advantages of Indian mercantile activity in the area similarly sought the immigration of Indians to help in the process of the development of Tanganyika. Though British authorities were not permitted but at least 600 labourers emigrated from the Portuguese port of Goa. The colonial government records indicate that another twenty one Indian artisans were recruited from Ajmer for service of the German East Africa railway.[8]

During the later half of the 19th century; the British were expanding their empire in Africa. To control the water way to India, after the completion of Suez, they needed their dominance over the Red Sea region. This required   transportation facilities to be developed to the interior. To achieve their colonial aims, the British undertook the task of constructing railways to connect Lake Victoria with the Indian Ocean at Mombasa.[9]

Before actually beginning the construction of the Railway, the government of British East Africa proposed to make a preliminary survey of the area, through which the projected rail lines were to run, with a view to make a rough estimate of the cost of the construction work. One hundred Sikh Soldiers were accordingly recruited from Punjab to protect those, who would be engaged in the reconnaissance work, from any possible hostility of the local tribes.[10] The actual construction work began with the African labour, which, however, was soon found to be neither enough nor continuous in supply. The government of India consequently encouraged recruitment of Indian labourers in East Africa.[11]

In January 1896, the first batch of 350 Indian labourers from the Punjab landed at the port of Mombasa, under the escort of R.P. Preston.[12] Despite initial difficulties, the recruitment of indentured workers for the Uganda Railway steadily increased after 1896 and continued till the competition of work. Although the number of Africans working on the railway never exceeded 2600, the total Indian employees rose from 3948 in 1896 to 6986 in 1897 and to 13003 in 1898. The high point occurred in March 1901 when 19742 Indians and 2506 Africans were employed. By Sep 1903, when the Uganda Railway committee was dissolved, 319883 indentured servants were imported for the railway works. Of these 16312 had been repatriated with the expiration of their contracts or through dismissal, 6454 had returned to India and 2493 had died. In March 1905 there were 1254 Indians still employed by the railway together with 53 Europeans, 176 Eurasians and 3050 Africans; and 436 of the Indians were still under contract.[13]

The importation of indentured Indians did not cease, with the completion of the trunk line from Mombasa to Kisumu in 1901 or the dissolution of the Railway Committee in 1903, Indians continued to be imported under contract until a new Indian emigration bill was enacted in March 1922.[14] The most important factor, for the attraction of Indians in this period, was the Indians who returned back and narrated stories of their vast opportunities in Africa. A certain number, together with friends and relatives, who could afford it, subsequently migrated at their own expense. The construction of the Uganda railway enhanced opportunities, to extend their trade activities in land. Indian commercial men and petty traders, whose ancestors had traded along the coast for generations and financed the caravan trade with the interior, followed the railway as it advanced towards the lake.

Large numbers of free immigrants augmented Indian population in this period. The crisis in India caused by the economic depression of the 1930s played an important role to pull immigrants to East Africa, where there were opportunities for employment in government service, crafts, commerce and wholesale and retail trade. In 1939, the Asian population in East Africa exceeded 100,000. Their number had increased both by a free flow of immigrants to East Africa for prospects of economic betterment, and by natural growth estimated at two to three percent per annum. By 1948

Kenya had a population about 97,000 Indians, Uganda 35,000, Tanganyika 46,000 and Zanzibar 16,000-the greatest proportionate increase since 1921 having occurred in Uganda. [15]

In the Post-World War II era there was an economic boom in East Africa. There was consequently a big increase in the demand for labour, leading to an up-gradation in the employment opportunities for the Asians. Such an upgradation in employment was facilitated by an enormous expansion in educational facilities. New primary and secondary schools sprouted in response to the governments *'Pound for Pound educational policy'*. Increase in fees and Indian education tax provided a source of increasing funds to pay for the building and running costs of the schools.[16] A policy of fee admission for Asian children from poor families gave education a more egalitarian face. South Asian parents in East Africa made enormous sacrifices in foregoing consumption and living frugally to create educational opportunities for their children. Asian children from East Africa went for tertiary studies to U. K., India and Pakistan and came back with technical and professional qualifications. From the late fifties three colleges in East Africa (Makerere College in Kampala, Royal College, which incorporated the Gandhi Memorial Academy, which had been built with Indian settlers funds, in Nairobi and the Administration and Law College in Dar-es-Salam) also provided opportunities.[17]

The burgeoning education industry needed teachers and these were sought in India, thus ensuring a continued expansion in the Indian population considerably above the natural rate of increase of around 2.2 per cent per annum. Ghai and Ghai estimate that by 1963 the Asian population in East Africa was placed at 372,000. The rate of increase between 1948 and 1963 was on average 4.2 per cent per annum.[18]

On the eve of independence the Asian population in East Africa was roughly estimated to be in between 372000 to 352100. According to A. Bharti in 1966 it was country wise- Tanzania 100000, Uganda 80000 and Kenya 182000 which in total comes around 362000.[19] But in post independent period Indian Diaspora faced tremendous crisis. Uganda's expulsion in the 1970s, Kenya's policy of discrimination and its 1982 riots and Tanzania's economic stagnation under anti capitalist policies, led to a sharp reduction in the Asian population in east Africa.

Issue of Identity of Indians in East Africa

Diversity among Indian Communities

The Indians in East Africa do not form a homogenous community but are comprised of a number of distinct subgroups. There is diversity in terms of religious beliefs as well as place of migration. Indians consists of Hindu, Sikh, Jain, Muslim, Christian, and Parsi beliefs while regionally they belong to mainly present Gujarat, Punjab and Goa states of India, though there are significant population of people from Maharashtra, Karnataka, Kerala, Tamil Nadu, Uttar Pradesh etc. W.T.W. Morgan writes about such diversity-

> "There is a deep cleavage between Hindus, Muslims and Goans and the first two contain many diverse communities within themselves. These have social, economic and geographical complications. Hindus are in the majority in Kenya and Uganda mostly being derived from the hinterland of Bombay and thus, speaking Gujarati. Sikhism is a reformed Hindu religion but in fact Sikhs are very distinct, speak a different language and have found a particular niche as mechanics, carpenters etc. (as well as adventurous drivers). Particularly the Sunni-Shia division divides Muslims. These communities are primarily religious but they tend to have their own language, newspapers, schools, clubs, societies, residential areas of towns and they marry within their own groups.[20]

Cultural practices

Members of the Indian Diaspora in East Africa are deeply conscious of their rich cultural heritage. They are aware that they are the inheritors of the traditions of the world's oldest civilization. They are keen to maintain their cultural identity. Deep commitment to their cultural identity has manifested itself in many ways and in every component of the Indians in East Africa. The earlier members of the Diaspora carried with them the rich traditions of harmonizing different customs, practices, values and beliefs. Kul Bhusan emphasizes on identity retention of Indians in East Africa as well as its impact on larger East African society. According to him:

"The skyline of every major town in East Africa is decorated with the graceful curves of a Hindu Temple, a Muslim Mosque or a Sikh Gurudwara. In Nairobi alone there are more than ten temples, six Gurudwaras and an equal numbers of Mosques. On the streets of most East African towns, Indian ladies lend a graceful touch with their colourful saris and other Indian fashions. In fact, most of the latest Indian fashions in saris and clothing are bought in local shops that have never a dearth of female clientele. And these are not enough. Indian foodstuffs were planted and they grew well here and sold in the green vegetable markets. Indian utensils and condiments and most other items of daily needs are available in a plentiful supply. And after an Indian meal at one of the many curry houses, the connoisseur may visit the "*Paan*" (betel) shop. To keep with the current events and trends in India, there are specialised bookshops-selling only Indian magazines that take only a few jet hours to reach Nairobi. Every Sunday the Indian newspapers for that day are available in Nairobi by lunchtime. A Gujarati weekly is published locally and another printed from Bombay has a special East African edition. In the 70's the voice of Kenya radio broadcasted 60 hours of Hindustani programmes every week. A great variety of music-classical, folk, film, popular was presented along with news and magazine programmes in Punjabi and Gujarati languages."[21]

It will be interesting to quote here Mr. R. P. Malaviya, then Attaché at the High- Commission of India in Nairobi, wrote on Feb. 23, 1962; in reply of A. Bharti, query about cultural and political leadership and about integration in the emergent African body politic. He wrote-

"The Indian community here has got the same cultural and social organizations as in India, e.g. the Arya Samaj, the Sanatan Dharma Sabha, the Sikh Union, Patel Brotherhood, Laohana Mandal, Surat District Association etc. They carry on their activities within these organizations. I have not come across any notable publications with regard to the cultural activities of Indians here; perhaps the need for such a publication has never been felt so for. Now with the coming of independence to these territories perhaps the greatest problem that will arise will be of the cultural and social integration of the Indians or to put it more precisely the Asian community with the indigenous people. As I mentioned before, since the communities are organized into various traditional social and cultural associations they have their own managing bodies besides which there is no special cultural leadership. Normally, the political leaders are also invited to important functions of these cultural organizations to preside over and address..."[22]

The issues of identity retention among Indians in East Africa have been examined in the seven parameters of culture viz. language, celebration of festivals, use of mass media, traditional cultural activities, religion, Sports, and food pattern.

Language

It is often said that 'unity in diversity' is soul of India. Indians in East Africa truly set example of above statement. There is diversity in terms of place of migration as well as language they speak. Regionally they belong mainly to present Gujarat, Punjab and Goa states of India, though there is significant population of people from Maharashtra, Karnataka, Kerala, Tamil Nadu, Uttar Pradesh etc. In lingual terms they are people who speak Gujarati, Punjabi, Hindi, Konkani etc. languages.

Kiswahili is the most common language of communication in East Africa and most of the urban educated population is well-versed in English language. Interestingly, People of Indian Origin have general understanding of both languages and use these languages for official purpose and while conversation with indigenous African. However, they prefer to speak languages of their motherland in home and while talking to other Indian people.

However, fluency in speaking Indian languages varies by generation of migration. As first generation migrants often consider Indian languages their mother tongue but second and third generations of Indian migrant community may not be as fluent in Indian languages. Gisbert Oonk also noted in his study of 'three generations' of Hindu Lohana in Tanzania. According to his analysis, the first generation of Hindu Lohana's went to East Africa during 1880-1920 from Gujarat. Most of them received at least their primary educations in their homeland. They were able to read, write, and speak Gujarati and some had a little knowledge of English when they arrived in East Africa. They preferred to use Gujarati language for their business purposes. The second-generation Hindu Lohanas in East

Africa were born in East Africa in the period between 1920 and 1960. They tried to retain their identity through preservation of lingual heritage and establish several 'Indian Schools' that would teach Indian languages Third generation Hindu Lohanas were raised in East Africa in the period 1960-2000. While Gujarati is still being spoken in conversation with elders, young generation speak to each other in English or Kiswahili. They have even forgotten to read and write Gujarati language.[23]

Celebration of Festivals

Celebration of festival is a very important way of identity retention. This is a universal phenomenon of mankind to celebrate festivals, nature of festivals and way to celebrate them varies from one social group to another The celebration of festivals is very much linked with their respective religions, like Hindu celebrate Diwali, Holi etc., Muslim celebrate Eid, Sikh Vaisakhi, Guru Nanak Jayanti, Parsi's Nowroj etc. People often celebrate those festivals in groups and normally common food is served on those occasions and everybody enjoys it. Sometimes they celebrate those festivals even in much bigger way than India.

Indians in East Africa celebrate festivals not only as a ritual but also highlight their socio-cultural importance and reasons to celebrate them. Often they enthusiastically link those with their motherland and feelings still attached with.

As date of Indian cultural festivals are based on there own calendars which does not fall same as Gregorian calendar, Indians publish their own calendars which give detailed information about date of festivals in Gregorian calendar. Nyanza Petroleum Dealers Limited, a company owned by ethnic Indian publishes its annual calendar focusing on any one aspect of Hindu culture.

Religion

Identity retention among PIOs in East Africa is probably most strong in terms of religion. Indian community in East Africa is multi-religious. There are followers of Hindu, Muslim, Sikh, Jain, Christian, Parsi, and Buddhist religion. Existing sects and sub-sects among Hindus (Arya Samaji, Sanatan Dharmi, Vaishnav, Shaiv etc.), Muslims (apart from Shia-Sunni sects there are Ismailis, Ithnaseris, Bohras and Ahmadiya sects), Sikhs (Namdhari and Ramgarhia), Jains (Swetambers and Digambers) are self explanatory to describe diversity of beliefs among them. Culture in the context of Indian Diaspora is virtually synonymous with religion. PIO's with few exceptions clung to their communal religions throughout their long residence in East Africa. Their religious orientation not only fragmented the community, but also affected their economic, political and social activity and determined their attitudes.

They celebrate their religious festivals, social functions and ceremonies as per customs and traditions of the religion which they belong. Any religious gathering is attended by huge number of people and usually it is not restricted to only people of same religious group. Rather people of other religious group and even indigenous people can attend and participate in those functions. So, it is not surprising to find people of Muslim community in the function of Arya Samaj or a Hindu visiting Gurudwara and offering prayer as other Sikhs.

Food Pattern

The identity retention of Indians in East Africa also reflects in their food pattern. Despite having their presence in the places where food habits are quiet different from those of India they have been able to maintain those same as Indians. Chapatti and rice remains their staple food and kitchens of every household among Indian community is full of spices, utensils, and other required material which completely looks like kitchen of any house in India. Indian food stuffs are fairly available in East African markets. Even in small cities like Kisumu, Eldorate Thika, Kitale, Kericho, Nyeri, Nanyuki, Machakos, Kisii, Meru, Kakamega, Gilgil, Fort Hall, Malindi, Embu, Lamu, Isiolo, Mtwara, Mikindani, Iringa, Mbeya, Mbale, Masaka, Soroti, Tororo, Iganga, Mbarara, Entebbe, Kamuli, Lira, Kebale, Gulu, Fort Portal, Arua etc. restaurants are serving Indian dishes. There are shops of Indian sweets, *chaat-papdi*, *chole-bhature*, *masala-dosa* etc. and not only ethnic Indians but also several indigenous people enjoy these delicious dishes every day. Balvinder Singh, manager of Ramgarhia Sikh Temple, Pangani who looks after *langar* (free meal service in the *Gurudwara*) informed that every required material for cooking of the meal is easily available in the local market.

Role, Status and Contributions of Indians

In-spite of this diversity one thing is common for all Indians and that is their contributions to the land of their new destiny. They have contributed positively to every stratum of East African economy, polity and society. They participated in national movement and made significant contribution in the nation building process. The success stories of entrepreneurs are legendary and they are playing a key role in industrialization process of the East Africa. From hi-tech manufacturing industries to traditional restaurants, from renowned hospitals to famous educational institutions, from popular games to leading think-tanks -everywhere contributions of Indians is visible which, is an obvious result of skill, dedication and hard work. The contributions of Indians in East Africa can be broadly outlined under three subheadings-economic, political and philanthropic activities.

Economic Contribution: Long association of Indians, led to tremendous contribution in East Africa which is most visible in economic terms. It is well accepted fact that East Africa was a difficult region in terms of human settlement as Gideon S. Wee and Derek A. Wilson points out "...There were large tracts of arid, waterless desert and semi-desert. There were areas dominated by the *Tse-Tse* fly and the Malaria carrying mosquito. There were the forested mountains and highland regions. There were the steep escarpments of the eastern and western rift valleys...."[24]

It was only Indians who could venture in internal land of East Africa and successfully operated their business and trade for centuries. But unlike British power they were concentrated on commercial activities and never tried to colonize the region. Later, in the colonial period many Indians went there as a victim and not as free commuter. First and foremost contribution of Indians during this period was construction of Railway link between Lake Victoria to Indian Ocean at Mombasa, commonly known as 'Ugandan Railway'. This was not an easy job, complexities and dangers involved in the work were well described by Lieut. Col. J.H. Patterson, then an engineer engaged on the construction of the Uganda Railway, in his book "The Man-Eaters of Tsavo and other East African Adventures"[25] Due to hard work, skills and dedication of indenture labours, 572 mile long railway link was completed within short span of time.

Equally important is contribution of Indians in the evolution of market system in East Africa. Indians were pioneer in the establishment of '*dukas*' (derived from the Gujarati word '*Dukan*' means a shop), local trading centers and bazaars in different localities. The introduction of a variety of imported items to the local population and later on the rupee as currency provided incentives for greater production as well as a transition from barter to money based economy.[26] They established their '*duka's*' in every corner of East Africa and there was a time when term '*dukawallah*' became synonymous for Indians. Despite several difficulties "*dukawallah*" carried the mechanism of monetary economy in the interior to create new methods in the process; he introduced a set of new values of mark for money, to produce for the market, to cultivate economic crops and to manufacture other goods not merely for exports but also for the expanding domestic market.[27]

However, post independence period has seen phenomenal change in this image. Successive governments of these countries imposed several restrictions on the involvement of the *alien* in local retail trading especially in remote areas. So majority of Indians moved to other options for their livelihood. Some of them entered in wholesale business or manufacturing sectors and made tremendous success. A major chunk of Indians joined private sector for employment as availability of government jobs for them was very difficult. A major chunk of Indians, who were professionally qualified, opted to work independently as architect, doctor, engineer etc. They all are contributing positively to the economy and society of East African countries as per their capacity.

Indians in East Africa are economically most successful community. On an average they are economically well off then their counterpart indigenous or European ethnic groups and firms like Chandaria, Madhvani, Manji, Chande and Mehta group etc. holds significant share in East African economy. Their entrepreneurship skills are well acknowledged by scholars. For instance, David Himbara, in his book "Kenyan Capitalists, the State and Development", writes about success of PIOs "Some of the determining factors that distinguished the Indians from businessmen in other Kenyan communities were their commercial skills, as evidenced by an ability to survive in remote areas on modest resources and by sheer determination and hard work; their vision of the potential mass market and the patience to transform it into an actual market; their general efficiency and competitive edge; and the role of family units and collective organizations in providing mechanism to engender discipline and cohesion."[28] Gijsbert Oonk refers to relatively better economic performance on Indian community, as 'when an African earns 20 dollars, he likes to live as he has earned 25 dollars. An Indian, however, will spend only 5 dollars and save 15 for further investment..."[29]

Legendry success in business and trade is also a big economic contribution to the country of adaptation. Indians are largest share holders in the revenues of Kenyan government as they pay taxes in various forms in Tanzania and Uganda too tax paying ratio of PIOs compare to their indigenous counterparts is much higher. They are bringing technological advancement in the country and most importantly they are one of the biggest employers of local population.

Political Contribution: Most of Indian immigrants went to East Africa for economic reasons. There were hardly any political motives involved in migration process. However, they made significant political contributions especially from the beginning of 20th century. Initially, they were united for the demand of better working conditions, then they begun protest against racial policies of colonial government. In later phase they participated in independence movement of their countries of adoption together with African leaders and played important role in the nation building process.

Role of PIOs in anti-colonial movement and nation building was historic. It is fairly acknowledged by scholars and East African political leaders. For instance Kenya's most respectable leader Tom Mboya said, "The overwhelming majority of the Indian community in Kenya, supported the African stand and wanted to adhere to the standards set by Nehru and Gandhi, as friend and allies in the struggle for freedom and democracy."[30]

However, after the independence of the countries in East Africa; the politics of racial hatred heightened. Since, Indian community constitutes even less than 1 percent of the total population; they have always been victims of this racial hatred. After attainment of independence many indigenous leaders in East Africa propagated that Asians have been brought there by colonial powers. And true independence can be only achieved by keeping Asians out from the political power and governmental situations. Under these circumstances, there were not many possibilities of participation in the country's political system. But despite these numerical disadvantages, PIOs have been able to show some achievements in the political systems of these countries. Political activities among the Indians of East Africa are pursued through associations such as Municipal Councils, town and district education boards, celebration and fund-raising committees, local branches of major political parties, and in some towns, employers associations. In these associations, Indian leaders represent the entire Indian community, on one hand, and the wider Afro-Asian community, on the other.[31]

PIOs are playing important role in the political sphere of Tanzania. There were many members of PIO community who could secure their place in parliament in different elections and in the government. If political participation or role of Indian Diaspora in these three countries of East Africa is compared, Tanzania is the country where Indian Diaspora has been more vocal in the political space and has secured place in different governments and political parties. For instance Mrs. Zakia Meghji as a finance minister of Tanzania has done remarkable contribution in the economic development and investment promotion in the country. According to country report of Ministry of External Affairs (India), in July 2005, a PIO Mrs. Shamim Parkar Khan was serving as a Deputy Minister of Tanzania and other 6 PIO's were member in the parliament.[32]

In Uganda despite ethnic Indians being wholeheartedly welcomed in the country, there was hardly any representation of ethnic Indians in the government machinery until 2001. In the June 2001, Jay Tanna, a Ugandan national of Asian origin was elected to represent the eastern region in the Ugandan parliament. Jay Tanna, whose family are investors in the eastern Ugandan town of Mbale, beat 20 rivals to be elected to represent young people in the eastern region. Tanna is the first Asian to be voted into office in some four decades

Indians have taken active part in numerous developmental and humanitarian activities in East Africa. Schools like Arya Boy's School, Arya Girl's School, Shree Sanatan Dharm School, Ismaili School, Goan School, Khalsa School, Allidina Visram High School, and Aga Khan Academy etc. are primarily established and funded by Indians and they are providing cheap and quality education to the children of Indians as well as to children of indigenous people. During the establishment of University of Nairobi, Indians were major contributor in terms of funds as well as intellectual resources. Apart from this Indians have established libraries such as Desai Memorial Library, Asian-African Heritage Trust Library, Oshwal Library, East African Ramgarhia Board Library etc. in various parts of Kenya with substantial collection of books and other resources. To provide proper and affordable medical facilities they have been running various hospitals, dispensaries and clinics such as M.P. Shah Hospital, Aga Khan Hospital, Parkland Nursing Home, Pandya Memorial clinic, Guru Nanak Hospital etc. They also organize Free Health Camps on different occasion. Asian Foundation, established by leading PIO businessmen is engaged in the enhancement of skills and employment opportunities for indigenous people.

Challenges faced by PIOs as a Minority Group

Though, 20th century witnessed large scale migration of Indians to East Africa, but their life in the country of adoption has not been smooth. In the colonial period they faced discriminatory practices of colonial government like, reservation of the Highlands for the Whites; official sponsorship of European immigration as against Indians; the grant of right of trial by jury to Europeans only and not the Indians; the legal exclusion of Indians from appointments as Justices of Peace; sale of certain township plots to Europeans only etc. They fought together with indigenous people against such practices and equally participated in national movement with the hope that once independence will be achieved their grievances will be shuttled. But, consequences of post independent period indicate that Indians have become more hated than Europeans.

From the very early days of independence, the issue of citizenship of Indians in East Africa remained very vital. It even led to a misunderstanding between Indians and indigenous community. It brought new political paraphernalia; even loyalty of Indians to their country of adoption was questioned. In order to clarify what exactly happened, it is necessary to discuss the issue in some detail. According to British government's decision, after the end of 1948 Indians were either British Subjects or British Protected Persons. The British subjects were Asians (including Goans) born on British territory (e.g. the former British India, Kenya Colony). Asians born in India's princely States in the Kenya Protectorate or in any other Protectorate or Mandated territories were, generally called British Protected Persons.[33]

On the eve of independence, Indian settlers were asked to opt, any one citizenship, among these three- Kenya, Uganda or Tanzania citizenship, British citizenship/subjects and Indian citizenship. Majority of Indians applied for British citizenship, and few of them applied for the citizenship of respective East African countries. But, those Indians who applied for the citizenship of their country of residence faced a deep silence of the government over their applications for citizenship. At the same time the government gave the impression that the Indians were unwilling to accept their citizenship.[34] Instead of looking at the root cause of such mindset and trying to short out grievances of Indians, African leaders utilized this opportunity to spread racial hatred.

Soon after independence, governments of these countries started the policies that were favourable to indigenous businessmen but anti-Indians. Indians faced a series of official and unofficial discriminatory policies in the 1960s-70s. These policies commonly called *Africanisation of the Economy*. Governments of East African states started restricting immigrants as well as non-citizens access to trade and work permits. When it realized that there were enough Indians with East African citizenship to frustrate African aspirations, the government switched to policy of *Africanisation* -which meant the cancellation or non-renewal of trading licenses to non-blacks, whatever their nationality was. Affirmative action in favour of the indigenous was apparent in every aspect of socio-economic life: in trade, the award of contracts, appointments to government jobs, and many other such spheres. President Kenyatta's repeated exhortations to Indians at public meetings to 'pack up and go' were taken literally and with British passports departed hastily to start a new life in the UK or North America.[35]

Situation was most vulnerable in Uganda during the period of Idi Amin. Dictator Idi Amin's announcement to expel Asians came on 9 August 1972; he wanted to see all Asians be out of Uganda within three months. According to Ugandan census report of 1969, there had been 74308 Asians in Uganda of which 25657, regarded themselves as Ugandan citizen but by the end of 1972 there were only few hundred PIOs were left in whole Uganda. PIO's were not only forced to leave behind own country but also harshly victimized. Keeping aside all the conventions of respecting for Human Rights and personal dignity of a human being, the departing PIO's were beaten up, the girls raped, and property including personal possessions and ornaments were forcibly taken from them by the country's military and police officers. Idi Amin, in a letter to the Secretary General of the United Nations, assured the world body that the Asians being expelled would be allowed to take their possessions and there would be no mistreatment of those leaving. In reality, each of expelled people was allowed to take out of the country no more than $ 131. A pecuniary limitation of $ 131 was placed on personal possessions they were allowed to take and many of them were made to leave behind valuable items like jewellery, cameras, tape recorders and radios. In the end, even those possessions which they were allowed to take out (and for which they paid excess baggage charges) did not all leave Uganda.[36]

Indians suffered heavily during the attempted military insurrection in 1982. This racial violence against Indians occurred during the August 1982 attempted coup, which was masterminded by Kenya's now disbanded Air Force. The attempted coup resulted in at least 145 deaths (all Africans) and about $ 120 million worth of damages (mostly to Indian business and property).

Section II

Strategic significance of Indian Diaspora in East Africa – an Assessment

Despite the difficulties Indian diaspora in East Africa faced they have been playing vital role in the socio-economic transformation of their land of destiny. Hard work, skills and passion have made them successful in entrepreneurship, services and other activities and they are sharing their economic prosperity with the needy people of the society by various philanthropic activities apart from generating significant revenue for the state. However, Indians as an economically integrated affluent immigrant community but socio - culturally aloof, have always invited racial animosity. Given this socio - economic political positioning of PIOs it is important see in what way how this affluent yet vulnerable diaspora could be used as a strategic asset by both sides for fostering bilateral relations and promoting economic engagement.

India has an edge compared to other external players in the region because of its diaspora. The fact that the Indian diaspora is deeply entrenched and spread across East Africa and knows its way around is a big advantage for India in terms of fostering sustainable partnerships. Many analysts and stakeholders believe that to take the India-East Africa relationship to the next level, re-engaging with the diaspora, a heritage resource is very important. In fact the large presence of the Indian diaspora in East Africa, can be an asset to both regions, as they occupy a vital strategic position, that links India with East Africa in a meaningful way. The resource can lessen cultural barriers and increase information sharing among people in both regions.

Having grown in stature economically and socially, the Indian diaspora are in a position to add value to advancement of the India-East Africa Partnership and can constitute strong allies in articulating India's strategic interest. They can act as ambassadors and improve diplomatic relations between the host and home countries. If the Indian diaspora in East Africa are galvanised, they can also play a role as valuable strategic actors in the implementation process of various development projects initiated by India and can strengthen India- Africa Partnership. There are great advantages to working cooperatively with the Indian diaspora in the translation of the Partnership policy priorities into feasible interventions and realisable actions. The Indian diaspora, for example, can fulfil rather specific roles in the process where gaps are left by other civil society organisations in both India and East Africa.

Apart from strengthening bilateral relations, it should be understood that the Indian Diaspora in East Africa can contribute to development and economic growth of its home country in much the same way, that they currently contribute to the economic welfare and development of their host countries. One can see instances of business houses similar to that of Indian business strengthening ties with India through possible joint ventures and increased trade through purchase of plant, machinery and various equipments from India as well as giving opportunities to Indian expatriates, who provide valuable skills in our business. However, while there is potential to use diaspora networks to facilitate business interests, yet the diaspora networks have not been used for advancing business.

The Indian government, however, has not really focused on the Indians in East Africa from economic point of view, which is why many of the big Indian business groups of Indian origin in that continent do not look at putting their money in India but instead tap business opportunities in Europe and America. However, if certain restrictions were eased and some steps are taken by the government, India could attract a lot of investment from this segment. Besides it could harness the vast knowledge and experience of the Indian business community in East Africa. Especially the local ground knowledge of companies could be tapped by Indian players looking at partnerships in the region.

There are many Indian business groups operating in East African countries. The big business houses from India such as the Tatas, Essar, Vedanta, and Kirloskar who are now operating in East Africa are in many cases engaged with the Indian diaspora there, including talented professionals of Indian origin. But somehow the broader links are not yet being built.

There seems to be a lack of policy level engagement by the Indian government particularly taking into account the uniqueness of this diaspora in East Africa, particularly their historical experiences. Their vulnerability is such that being a minority any visible attempt to foster external loyalties, however innocuous it may be for domestic system, could invite suspicion and hostility, if done without taking the local leaders into confidence. Now since the East African countries are devising diaspora policies to engage their own diaspora, which is spread across the world for fostering development partnerships, the potential of Indian diaspora can be explored by both host and home countries to promote sustainable partnerships.

At present opportunities lies in their rising prosperity, their business, technical skills, their industry, enterprise, their willingness to collaborate with India and the value given in developing a diaspora network in business, technology, culture and education. India therefore needs to recognize the strategic significance of Indian diaspora in East Africa as a heritage resource.

End Notes

1   For earlier estimate see PC Jain "Indians Abroad: A current Population Estimate" Economic and Political Weekly" 17 (8) 1982. The recent figure has been compiled nom different sources: - *Europa World Year Book* and other Region and Country specific year books.

2   Government of India, 2001, *Report of the High Level Committee on the Indian Diaspora* ,New Delhi: ICWA, P .94

3   Daniel D.C. Don Nanjira, *The Status of Aliens in East Africa* (New York: 1976), p.3.

4   Robert G.Gregory, *India and East Africa: A History of Race Relations within British Empire, 1890-1939*, (London: 1971), p.40.

5   Ibid. pp.12-13.

6   J.S. Mangat, *A History of Asians in East Africa c. 1886-1945* (London: 1969), p.28.

7   F.D. Lugard, *Rise of our East African Empire* (London: 1893) pp.488-89.

8   J.S. Mangat, *A History of Asians in East Africa c. 1886-1945* (London: 1969), pp.30-31.

9   George Delf *Asians in Uganda* (London 1963), p.2.

10   H.P. Chattopdhayaya, *Indians in Africa* (Calcutta: 1970), p.335.

11   Ibid. p.335. ; H.S. Morris, *Indians in Uganda* (London: 1068), p.8.

12   H.P. Chattopadhyaya, *Indians in Africa* (Calcutta: 1970), p.333.

13   Robert G.Gregory, *India and East Africa: A History of Race Relations within British Empire, 1890-1939,* (London: 1971), p.52.

14   H.S. Morris, *Indians in Uganda* (London: 1068), p.9.

15   J.S. Mangat, *A History of Asians in East Africa c. 1886-1945* (London: 1969), p.140.

16   Ibid. pp.173.

17   D.P. Ghai and Y.P. Ghai, ed., *Portrait of a minority: Asians in East Africa* (London: 1965), p. 102.

18   Ibid pp. 127-28.

19   A. Bharti, *Asians in East Africa Jayhind and Uhuru* (Chicago: 1972), p.20-21.

20   W.T.W. Morgan, 1973, *East Africa,* London, Pp.152-53.

21   Kul Bhusan, P. 128.

22   A. Bharti, 1972, *Asians in East Africa: Jayhind and Uhuru,* Chicago: Nelson Hall, Pp. 175-76.

23   Gisbert Oonk, 'We Lost our Gift of Expression-Loss of the Mother Tongue among South Asians in East Africa, 1880-2000', in Gijsbert Oonk (ed.),2007, *Global Indian Diasporas,* Amsterdam: Amsterdam University Press, Pp. 67-88.

24 Gideon S. Wee and Derek A. Wilson, 1974,*East Africa through a Thousand Years,* London , P. 5

25 Patterson J.H., 1919,*The Man-Eaters of Tsavo and other East African Adventures,* London.

26 Niranjana Desai, 'Asian influence in East Africa' in J.K. Motwani, Mahin Gosine and J.B. Motwani ed.,op.cit, P. 127.

27 R.R. Ramchandani, 1976, *Uganda Asians: The End of an Enterprise,* Bombay p.90.

28 David Himbara, 1994, *Kenyan Capitalists, the State and Development,* Nairobi, p. 35.

29 Oonk Gijsbert, 2006, 'Towards a Historical Explanation of the Economic Success of a Middlemen Minority', *Awaaz* Issue III, P.8.

30 A.R. Pathak, xxxiii, P. 53.

31 Daniel D.C. Nanjira, 1976, *The Status of Aliens in East Africa,* New York: Praeger Publishers. Pp. 110-12.

32 ---*Country Report- Tanzania,* Ministry of External Affairs, India, July 2005 , Accessed 22 October 2006, www. mea.gov.in.

33 C. Singh, 1971, 'The Problems of Citizenship' in Aniruddha Gupta, ed., *Indians Abroad: Asia and Africa,* New Delhi, P. 176.

34 A. Gupta, 'The Asians in East Africa: Problems and Prospects,' *International Studies,* 1968-69 Pp. 280-81.

35 *Report of the High Level Committee on Indian Diaspora,* op.cit, P. 98.

36 K.C. Kotecha, 1975, 'The Shortchanged: Uganda Citizenship Laws and how they were Applied to its Asian Minority', *The International lawyer,* Vol. 9, No. 1, January ,, P. 3

Chapter - 5

Security Challenges in East Africa: India's Cooperation for Stability

Introduction

India's growing relations with East Africa is one that depicts the changed international security environment and conflict landscape. The changing dynamics in international security coupled with the limited resources for peace operations, have motivated nations, regions and the international community to form partnerships to respond to a rapidly changing peace and security environment characterized by terrorism, piracy, and political upheavals, often leading to complex emergencies. The increasingly blurred line between international security and domestic security has led the international community to engage more frequently into domestic conflicts. In Africa in general and East Africa in particular the severity of these security threats have been a key factor in the revival of partnerships and the promotion of the associated concept of cooperation with international actors which includes India. Peace and security actors in Africa have not been reluctant in engaging international stakeholders in building capacity for peace operations.

The African Union particularly has been instrumental in enhancing cooperation with the United Nations and European Union on various aspects of peace security and development. For instance, when the AU was established in 2002, one of its key mandates and/or primary responsibilities was that of maintaining international peace and security on the continent. Even after inauguration of AU's Peace and Security Council (PSC) in 2004, it is still obvious that the continent lacks sufficient prerequisites to enable it act as an efficient conflict manager. Notably, the Africa Union lacks the capacity to carry out peace and conflict management operations in Africa unless it gets financial, logistical and technical support from the international community. In circumstances where a financial facility exists on the continent such as the African Peace Fund (APF), the conditionalities seem to greatly narrow down opportunities for promoting the concept of 'African solutions to African problems.'

As far as India is concerned it has been contributing to the peace and development of Africa in its own capacity. Particularly in East Africa the growing relations suggest that in the coming years, peace and security cooperation will be further strengthened. Given India's enormous stake in the region maintaining peace and stability not only is in the interest of the East African region but also for India's own interest from the perspective of furthering a long-term relationship with the region.

The region forms a part of India's strategic maritime frontiers, which extend from the Persian Gulf to the east coast of Africa and across to the Malacca Strait. The significance of the region to India's economic development and security is immense. Most of India's trade is by sea and nearly 89 per cent of India's oil is supplied through sea.[1] Protection of sea lanes of communication in the Indian Ocean' is vital for India's economy to avoid any disruption in flow of trade and oil supply. This was emphasized by Prime Minister Manmohan Singh in a joint press conference with Mozambique's President Armando Guebuza in New Delhi in September 2010, wherein he stated that: 'It is our common mutual interest to ensure the safety and security of sea lanes of communication in the Indian Ocean'. In this context Indian Ocean littorals and the Eastern African countries in particular hold special place.

Indian's President's visit to Tanzania in 2004, which led to an agreement for increased training of Tanzanian military personnel in India and more frequent calls by Indian warships at Tanzanian ports, indicates the strategic importance of East African countries to India. Maritime relations have been expanding with East African countries. According to an Indian naval official:

> With India's economic interest in West Africa and Asia region increasing, Navy will be playing its diplomatic role by visiting more ports all along the coast of eastern Africa, touching the Horn of Africa ... Most of the navies in eastern Africa are small in size compared to the Indian Navy. What we would be aiming during these interactions is to give them the confidence that India would come to their aid whenever there is a need, considering that we have enough experience in all aspects of operations, be it military, diplomatic, policing or benign. [2]

While maritime security challenges has made India to reach out to East African counties for maintaining peace and security in the Indian Ocean region, greater focus is also being laid on cooperating with East African countries for achieving security and stability in the East African region. The region, in the recent years has been witnessing various security challenges, which is having implications for growth and development. In this Chapter an attempt has been made to analyze the burgeoning cooperation between East African states and India from security and peace perspective. It analyzes various security challenges that the region is confronted with and the responses to such challenges by the regional community, the East African countries and India. It also examines the potential areas of cooperation between India and East Africa for promoting peace and stability in the region.

Security Challenges in East Africa

In the East Africa region, comprising Kenya, Uganda, Tanzania, Rwanda and Burundi, the states in the Community are relatively young, having achieved their independence in the early 1960s. They have similarities in political, economic and social terms. Politically, they have experienced in varying degrees, forms of authoritarian rule and have undergone democratic transformations beginning in the early 1990s. Economically, they have experienced stagnation and marginalization. However, currently there is a turn around, with each recording positive growth. Socially, they are heterogeneous and are faced with identity based fault lines which in different times have led to violent ethno-political conflicts. In the extreme, Rwanda and Burundi have been sites of ethnocide.[3]

The political, social and economic experiences have had a negative impact on security in its multidimensional and interactional character. This is because states have either generated insecurities or have been so emasculated to the extent that their infrastructural, despotic and legitimating power is marginal, and incapable of delivering holistic development which is central in enabling and enhancing security. [4]

The region, at present is mired with various security challenges ranging from terrorism, maritime security, human security, and inter- state divergences owing to resource and infrastructure securitization. These challenges have grave implications for regional stability. An examination of these security challenges and the responses is crucial to have an understanding of security scenario in the present context.

Terrorism in the East African Region

Historically East African countries have been soft targets for international terrorism from the 1970s to date. During that time these countries did not have clear strategies and plans for tackling the issue, nor was terrorism prioritized in the security agenda. The security agencies in the region were also ill-equipped and not trained to deal with the issue. The awakening only came with the August 1998 bombings of the two American embassies in Kenya and Tanzania. Since then the region has been littered with many counterterrorism initiatives at the national and regional levels. Since 2003 the regional countries have been formulating and establishing mechanisms and programmes to address the institutional weakness that hinder their counter-terror activities.[5] The countries have also defined terrorism as a common threat facing the countries, and efforts to seek common strategies to address the issue have started, however with limited progress.

Prior to the 1998 bombings of the American embassies in Kenya and Tanzania, the East African Community states were not committed to implementing existing regional and international legislations on terrorism. The attacks awakened firstly, the Organisation of African Unity's (OAU) — later the African Union's (AU) — resolve to address the threat of terrorism through the 1999 OAU *Convention on the Prevention and Combating of Terrorism* (Algiers Convention). Secondly following the revival of the EAC in 2000 the Community embarked on the development of a Draft EAC Protocol on Peace and Security in which terrorism is identified as one of the threats facing the region. Alongside the EAC Treaty, the Community developed a strategy on peace and security. The Community has also developed enabling frameworks to address issues of security at large including terrorism. The EAC frameworks on conflict prevention and management and on conflict early warning and response when and if fully operationalized will assist the member countries address the threat of terrorism.[6]

There are various reasons as to why East African region has been a target of international terrorism. These include proximity to the fragile Somalia state, inadequate counter terrorism strategies, poor governance, poverty and employment factors that have been exploited by terror networks. The region is also characterized by intractable conflicts that have resulted in an increase in the number of refugees who move across the porous borders with firearms and explosives, specifically in and out of Somalia and across the East African countries. Some of the refugees have links to radical Islamic ideas and at times are sympathetic to their relatives who have been recruited and indoctrinated in terrorist ideals.[7]

The region has seen rise of radicalized Muslim elements having close linkages with external terrorist networks and safe havens access with their Muslim brothers in the region. They use the mosques and religious activities to draw sympathizers and recruits for their activities.[8] The susceptibility of the region to such terror acts sponsored by Al Shabab group in Somalia, may also be attributed to the countries' involvement in stabilization efforts in Somalia and due to close ties with countries that have interests in the region such as Israel, USA and European countries, which further contribute to the vulnerabilities in the region as their interests are often targeted for attack.

Despite the international dynamics of terrorism in the EAC region, the underlying causes are rooted in the domestic grievances and circumstances of the perpetrators. Even strong support bases in the region protect individuals and organizations from local communities, and allow attacks to be easily planned and executed. Sometimes perceptions regarding counter-terrorism strategies being targeted at specific communities or religions generate feeling within such communities that their identity is under attack, and thus breed support for terrorist activities. In some instances indoctrination of vulnerable populations are successful, owing to high levels of poverty and unemployment prevalent in the region. In other instances the counter terrorism strategies in the region have acted as a push factor that has hardened the resolve of some extremists to engage in terrorist activities. The ease of entry and exit through the porous borders and the safety with which individuals and groups can move in the region makes it vulnerable.

In the recent past mostly terror attacks have been executed mainly in Kenya, Uganda and Tanzania, with Kenya being the most frequent target. Burundi and Rwanda have mainly experienced terror challenges from local national actors, which are beginning to gain a regional dimension. Somalia is considered the main source of the terrorist threat, particularly the *Al Shabaab* terror group that has links with *Al Qaeda*. The main reason why these countries are targeted is because of their role in stabilization initiatives in Somalia and the region. Recent threats have targeted the

AMISOM troop contributing countries of Burundi and Uganda who have suffered casualties in and out of Somalia, and lately Kenya for its military operations against the *Al Shabaab* militias following several incursions into its territory.[9]

Members of the Somali ethnic community were initially the main perpetrators, and with large refugee population having spread out across the East African countries, it becomes easier for the terrorists to move across the region. Recently other ethnic communities in the region have begun to participate in terror activities, further complicating counter terrorism strategies.[10]

Regional Responses to Terrorism

The growing terrorism in the East Africa has enhanced state and regional responses with the creation of counter-terrorism strategies both at the regional and national levels of East African countries. At the domestic level various countries have adopted various counter-terrorism initiatives involving local measures. There have been efforts by states in the region to establish multi-agency or national counter-terrorism centres that comprise all security agencies, immigration agencies and other stake holders to act as focal points for their counter terrorism initiatives. These centres are expected to work closely with regional and international initiatives set up to counter the threats in the region. [11].

The countries in East Africa have also imposed strict immigration rules and procedures at their entry points to prevent the free movement of suspect persons across the states. There is also growing closer cooperation on issues of immigration as evidenced in EAC provisions that include the introduction of the EAC travel passport. Border surveillance, training, and modernization programmes for equipment and technology are also taking place across the states.[12]

The EAC countries have utilized international assistance as a strategy. Since 1998 the region has been receiving support and cooperation from several western states and the United States of America (USA). The support received from these, however, has made the countries more vulnerable to terror attacks, as they are perceived to be sympathetic propagators of the Western' agenda. Terrorist groups in the region are known to target western and American interest in the respective countries. Other strategies undertaken by regional countries include transforming the security apparatus to be able to respond to counter terrorism, policing and administration initiatives and general sensitization activities for the public to create awareness of the threat of terrorism.[13]

The EAC Draft Protocol on Peace and Security states that the EAC states will jointly formulate strategies and mechanisms to combat terrorism conduct joint operations, and counter terrorism, which shall also be implemented in the context of African Union (AU) and United Nations Agreements. Terrorism remains an issue of concern to both EAC states and India. There are however opportunities to work together to be able to address some elements of the threat more specifically those which are common to both.

Human Security challenges in East Africa

Drawing on Ayoob's argument that Africa's security threats are primarily internal, this section focuses on analyzing the key foundational internal security challenges facing the region (Ayoob, 1991). Essentially, it focuses on generators of deprivation since this best captures all those aspects which lead to exclusion, poverty, and decline in capability formation, human welfare, and physical violence. These deprivations undermine stateness and human security. In earlier section it was discussed how such deprivations sometimes become a root cause for terrorism and other forms of political violence. The challenges are analyzed below.

Inadequate Access to Education breeds Insecurity

Education is one of the most powerful instruments for enhancing security. This is because it has a multiplier effect. It leads to capabilities formation, which enables individuals and groups to constructively deal with the challenges facing them[14]. Education enables individuals to break the poverty cycle, better address public health challenges and adopt relevant knowledge and technologies capable of enhancing the foundational requirements for achieving security.

In East Africa, states have made tremendous efforts in enhancing access to basic education. The primary school enrolment rate is above 90 per cent, and governments are committed to enabling free access to primary school level. Also, the region enjoys an average of 70 per cent literacy level. However, it is plagued by a low transition rate to secondary education and higher education institutions. In Burundi, the secondary enrolment rate is 15.6 per cent, 29.9 per cent in Tanzania, 23.0 per cent in Uganda and Rwanda, and 32.0 per cent in Kenya. In higher or tertiary education, the enrolment rates are well below 7 per cent. Considering that access to secondary and higher education is critical to realizing the empowering benefits of education, the region faces severe and inadequate access to education.[15]

Health Insecurity

Lack of or inadequate access to health services impacts on security in multiple ways at micro and macro-levels. At the micro-level, sickness and loss of lives lead to depletion of income and poverty[16]. For instance, sickness of the household breadwinner could lead to reduced consumption, lack of access to education by dependents, sale of assets and depletion of family savings, sinking households into poverty. At the macro-level, poor health leads to decline in productivity, and huge expenditure reducing the finances available for investment in other sectors, and undermines state security.

In East African countries, health infrastructure is extremely weak. Access to health is limited because of unavailability of health services in terms of geographical coverage, low doctor-patient ratios, unaffordable costs of treatment and drugs, lack of information on preventive health, and dependency on the importation of expensive pharmaceutical products.

There is high prevalence of diseases especially HIV/AIDS, tuberculosis and malaria in the region. According to 2010 data, the HIV/AIDS prevalence rate stood at 3 per cent in Burundi, 2 per cent in Rwanda, and 6 per cent in Tanzania, Kenya and Uganda. Malaria, which is a highly preventable disease, has remained the main killer in the region. In Kenya, 20 per cent of all deaths of children under 5 years were as a result of malaria. Overall, 26,077 deaths from malaria were reported. In Tanzania, malaria killed 15,876, in Uganda 3,431, and in Burundi, 2,667.[17] Regarding TB, higher incidence rates have been reported in 2010. There were 120,000, 79,000 and 70.000 new cases in Kenya, Tanzania and Uganda respectively. These diseases are compounded by the high prevalence of communicable diseases especially diarrhoea, typhoid and cholera which are a result of poor sanitation. Further, the region suffers from low life expectancy ranging from 50 years in Burundi to 55 years in Tanzania.

Such health insecurity and poverty negatively reinforce one another with disastrous consequences. It not only retards development but also affects the stability of the region by making the overall security condition more precarious.

Food insecurity

Food security is a fundamental need, basic to all human needs and organization of social life. It is the assurance of access to adequate nutrition, either through direct effort or exchange at acceptable prices. More so, it means access to necessary nutrients which is key to not only life, but also to a stable and enduring social order.[18] Essentially, food security is central to other human, societal and state endeavours.

Despite having the potential to feed itself and generate surplus for export, East Africa is a food deficit region. Its low productivity, high food prices and supply constraints have left millions without food and adequate nutritional requirements. Majority of farmers who are engaged in subsistence agriculture have a productivity level which is a third of their potential. The region has experienced price volatility, in food prices. For instance, in 2011 prices skyrocketed by more than 100 per cent. Since the majority of the population is either below or barely above the poverty line, a large percentage of their income is spent on food and any surge in prices forces them to either cut down on dietary intakes or fail to pay for other needs such as education and health.

A review of the data indicates the extent of food insecurity. In Uganda, a 2004 study showed that malnutrition causes 40 per cent of deaths among children, 38 per cent suffer from studded growth, and 25 per cent of children below five are underweight. Further the goitre rate stood at 58 per cent for children between 6 and 11 years and 50 per cent of young women suffered from iron deficiency anemia, which is a major cause of maternal deaths.[19] Overall, in 2010, more than 1.2 million people were on the verge of starvation. In Kenya an estimated 3.75 million people were faced by starvation in 2011.

In Tanzania, 40 per cent of the population lives in chronic food deficit regions. In Burundi, only 28 per cent of the population is food secure, and has a cereal deficit of between 350,000 to 500,000 metric tons. Overall, the reunion measures poorly in food security. In Gross Hunger Index, Burundi measures 40 per cent, Rwanda 25.4 per cent, Tanzania 21.2 per cent, Kenya 20.2 per cent, and Uganda 14.8 per cent. All these measures are categorized as alarming.[20]

Violent conflicts

The region has experienced violent conflicts driven by ethno-political competition, natural resources scarcity and militant cultures. With the exception of Tanzania, all the other states in East Africa have witnessed mass violence. In Kenya, there has been ethno-political driven violence, which has manifested during the election process. The 2007-2008 elections is a case in point. The violence that erupted during that time almost transformed into a civil war. By the time peace was restored, more than 1.000 lives had been lost, half a million displaced, and sources of livelihoods destroyed.[21] Further, Kenya also suffered low intensive conflict in pastoral regions, driven by commercial and cattle rustling. In addition it has seen militarization of natural resources owing to rivalry and competition, especially on land and pasture.

In Uganda, the 2011 elections witnessed low intensity violence with the electoral commission identifying nine political party militias.[22] Additionally, the state has faced insurgencies in its northern region. The insurgency by the Lords Resistance Army (LRA) has led to thousands of deaths and displacements and widespread poverty.[23] Also it is observed that cattle rustling have resulted in violence in the Karamoja region.[24] In Rwanda and Burundi, there has been large scale ethnocide in the past decade which left more than a million massacred.[25] In Tanzania, which has largely escaped large scale violence except in Zanzibar, which has had cycles of ethno-religious/nationalism violence, the heightened political competition and increased penetration of capitalism is presently leading to nascent polarisation along ethnic lines. Such polarisation cannot be overlooked since Tanzania is the most diverse state in the region, with over 250 ethnic groups.

Though violent conflicts which the region has experienced are presently not there, yet the propensity for such conflicts remains, as the root causes still persists.

Infrastructure for Resource Securitization: Resultant Insecurity

The states in East Africa, which were designed and carved out by the Colonial powers, are endowed with different assets. Some are advantaged by energy and water resources, but are challenged by access to the Ocean such as Uganda. The opposite is true for littoral states, which have less energy resources but have a communication infrastructure in place like Kenya and Tanzania. Given the apparent security related dependencies, these have been developing into apparent mutual insecurities. State endowed with vertical infrastructure benefit from the dependency of those without. However at same time they become sensitive when these dependent states look for alternate exits and unilateral measures for securitisation of their resources. It generates insecurity due to loss incurred, lost prestige and reduced ability to influence events on land. Such insecurities related to infrastructure and securitization of resources sometimes generates tensions between states, with having propensity towards conflict. One example is Sudan and South Sudan case, wherein South Sudan is looking for alternate exits for its oil supply to avoid being dependent on Sudan for oil transport through pipeline running through its country. Mistrust, lack of information, regional anarchy and the availability of external capital is likely to create power struggles. This demonstrates how geography mediates political interactions among states affirming the link and causal relationship between political power and geographical space.

For instance one of the vertical infrastructure threats was the disputed 2007 elections in Kenya, when the entire Great Lakes region was locked down for infrastructure disruptions. If colonial cartographers designed Kenya as a convergence of multiple racial, religious, and ethnic fault-lines, economic and political policies now mediated its emergence as a strategic fulcrum and junction of the East Africa, Horn of Africa and Great Lakes sub-systems. This further adds to its classical centrality in the dormant but geo-politically critical Indian Ocean sub-system. Fear that is inherent in such kind of dependency by regional states gets animated with the discoveries of resources. Resources have created attempts by both revisionist and *slant quo* states like Uganda and Tanzania respectively, to seek alternative infrastructure that can enable them to access more value out of their resources, thus effectively generating friction with Kenya.

Uganda and Tanzania rejected any option of processing their oil and gas in Kenya. They opted to build their own energy infrastructure in favor of value addition. Uganda sought to construct a new oil refinery with a production capacity of 4000 bpd to take advantage of the estimated 200000 bpd production by 2015. The objective was to produce heavy fuel for power production, at 156,000 metric tons of fuel and 32000 metric tons of white products per year. This underpinned the drive for energy security to assuage the 11000 bpd of fuel or 580000 cubic meters per year consumed in Uganda, which increases by 3.5 to 5 per cent annually. Uganda's drive is to produce fuel for both domestic and regional consumption. Its initial mindset was on Kenya's 55,000bdp consumption in addition to Rwanda, Burundi, Eastern DRC and South Sudan. It sought to have Tallow and Heritage companies build a $ 2bUS pipeline to Mombasa for export. This orientation caused several insecurity fears based on the apparent dependence Kenya had on the Ugandan market and by inference Rwanda, Burundi and Eastern Congo. Uganda remains a leading consumer of Kenya's oil at 30 per cent of all exports. Any unilateral exit from this is likely to affect Kenya negatively from the lost tax revenues accrued from profits to Kenya pipeline, road transport companies, and import export firms to exports of oil products. For Kenya, threats also lie in the imagined possibility of a successful decoupling of Rwanda, Burundi and DR Congo from its energy infrastructure.[26]

Uganda is also seeking to increase its level of strategic flexibility with the road and rail network by seeking a joint project with Tanzania to build a rail, pipeline and road linking the port of Tanga to Port Bell on Lake Victoria through Arusha, Musoma, and Kampala, thus adding insecurity. China Civil Engineering Corporation completed the project feasibility study in 2012. The projected estimated to cost $3billion includes an 880 km rail, Mwambani port in Tanga, a port at Fort Bell and Musoma docks. There will be rail connections from Tororo to Gulu 600 km away before connecting to Juba through a 250km line and an additional 550 km line to Wau in Southern Sudan.

Tanzania seeks to put up a 1,150 km pipeline from Dar-es-Salaam to Mwanza to provide Uganda with an alternative outlet. Tanzania equally signed an agreement with Rwanda and Burundi for the construction of a railway from Bagamoyo through central Tanzania beginning from 2014 at the cost of $4.7b. Motivated partly by inefficiencies in Mombasa port and the post-election chaos in Kenya in 2007, Rwanda and Burundi seek to increase their flexibility by negotiations with Tanzania to set up a rail link through central Tanzania to Bagamoyo. Tanzanian argues that it would decouple these states from Mombasa.

Kenya has evolved plans to establish a faster rail network at a cost of 320 billion shillings (S4billion) to cover 1300km from Mombasa to Malaba in effect targeting the Great Lakes. It has also embarked on a new transport corridor from Lamu. It will have connections to Addis Ababa and Juba from Isiolo junction. China agreed to fund the construction of facilities that include rail, road, pipelines, port and refinery. It is estimated that Kenya would earn as much as 7.5 billion shillings annually to transport 2.5 million tones of South Sudan's oil. The significance of this corridor increased with the breakout of conflicts between the two Sudans. Indeed once the project was initiated by the presidents of Ethiopia, South Sudan and Kenya, North Sudan send a pretest note to Kenya accusing it of endangering its national security and undermining regional security.

Such approaches being state-centric, they are likely to underpin geo-political tension among these states. The net result is likely to be insecurity and security dilemmas, as each state's actions are (mis) interpreted as hostile thus necessitating opposite and equal responses

This analysis of the salient security challenges in East Africa is not exhaustive. However, it captures the major security challenges which lead to impairing growth and development and thus instability of the region. The argument is that access to education and health, food security absence of physical violence, political violence, maritime insecurity and religious extremism, are key determinants of productivity, development and general well being. This in turn strengthens the foundation of security.

What is pertinent to understand is that the security challenges that the region faces is extremely complex. Any response to the challenges, whether at the national, regional and international level therefore takes into cognizance the complex form of security crisis in the region. In this context it is important to understand the various forms of complex security crisis in the region

Complexity of Security Crises

The complex security crises in East Africa are outcome of the internal cultural, political and socio-economic dynamics in the region having linkages basically to internal and external conflicts within any delineated geographical boundaries. Ideally, the 1990s genocide in Rwanda, the outcome of religious extremism of the youth (Al Shabaab) groups in the Horn of Africa, the inhuman activities by guerilla warlords such as Joseph Kony and his Lord's Resistance Army (LRA) in northern Uganda, and the ethnic enmity that the Eastern Africa sub-region witnessed during elections are some cases in point while referring to complex security emergencies in the region.[27]

Contemporary East Africa is stuffed with several regional security complexes. Ideally, the complexity is defined based on the group of states whose primary security concerns interact sufficiently closely that their individual national securities cannot realistically be considered in isolation or without taking into account the security of the others. For example, the more than two decades political instability in Somalia has become a trans-boundary problem affecting virtually all the countries not only in the Horn of Africa but also those that contribute troops for peace enforcement from the East Africa region such as Burundi and Uganda.

There are a number of interrelated issues that define the complex peace and security in East Africa. States are differentiated in terms of security threats, both internal and external, impact of non-state actors, external actors and the level and intensity of intra-regional security interdependence. They are locked in geographical proximity with each other, which often creates the drive and propensity for establishing regional organizations and collective security mechanisms. The geographical proximity and other factors such as socio-cultural, historical, racial, linguistic, ethnic, religious similarities and ideological perceptions, also induce patterns of mutual security interdependence or vulnerability, of amity in terms of friendship and dependable expectations of peaceful co-existence, and enmity in terms potentially hostile, suspicious and distrustful relationships. Geographical proximity and interactions amongst states in a specific geographical area inevitably bind the states and peoples together in a common security framework with distinct perceptions of collective threats to security and feelings of vulnerability. For example, the common perception in the Eastern African sub-region is the view that disarming armed bandits in one country is a serious threat to the very survival of the other neighbouring country-hence feelings of mutual vulnerability. The oscillating disarmament, demobilization and re-integration (DDR) programmes among the border communities in northern Kenya and eastern Uganda serve to indicate the complexity of sub-regional peace and security.

In the region, the intertwining nature of conflicts, the spillover effects of disaster occurrences and multiple security threats make it evident communities in the region are locked in a regional security complex.[28]. The states and peoples are bound together such as to share common military, security, political and ethno-religious security threats. For instance, the military security of the Tutsi in Burundi is linked to the security of the

Tutsi in Rwanda. Equally, the national security and political stability of Somalia is now inextricably linked to the security and stability of neighbouring Djibouti, Ethiopia, Eritrea, Kenya, Tanzania, Burundi, Rwanda and Uganda. Cross-border resource-based conflicts in most of these countries replicate each other in pattern, trend and demands. There are countless actors both foreign and local that continue to manipulate the region that continues to hinder the peace process in East Africa. Al-Shabaab continues to wreaking havoc not only in Somalia, but also with their recruitment within Kenya proves to detrimental to society, thus achieving its geopolitical strategies within the region. However, geopolitics in East Africa can have positive outcomes as well. At the moment, Kenya is busy training South Sudanese officials and diplomats to handle the new bureaucracy and diplomatic challenges, which will bring stability to the region if it is achieved in a successful and timely manner. On the other hand, countries like Uganda, Burundi, Rwanda, and Eastern Congo "have geo-political interests in Kenya's stability as the gateway to the sea, or as the strongest political economy in the region. To them, peace and stability in Kenya translates to a sense of comfort in the neighbourhood because it has been the place to run when things go wrong elsewhere"[29]. The geopolitics in East Africa are complicated and tightly interwoven which can easily disrupt the peace and security in the region overnight, or it could bring positive changes if used in a constructive way.

It is obvious that response to these complex scenarios presents problems and diverse challenges. Also, the phenomenon of complex political crisis characterizes the complexity of peace operations in many parts of Africa, more so Eastern Africa. It is important to note that in complex political crisis there is clear departure from conventional military security forces and involves civil militias, child soldiers and paramilitary forces. Analysts have described them as wars of attrition which become not only an extension of politics by other means, but also an extension of exploitation of war economies and struggle for access and control of state resources.[30] Indeed, previous politico-economic studies have revealed that majority of these conflict-torn societies are peripheral economies, and the inefficient political and economic management of the state has undermined its capacity to provide welfare and security.[31] Therefore, the complex political crisis is a continuum describing the conditions immediately before, during and after conflict or escalations of hostility, and requiring immediate intervention or response.[32]

The features of a complex political crisis known for its violent conflicts, atrocities, genocide and multiplicity of actors obviously require a Rapid Deployment Capability (RDC). East Africa, like any other developing country, suffers resourcing challenges to effectively respond to such emergencies. But, previous experiences by UN reveal shows that scaling up peace operations to an international profile mitigates some of the financial and logistical bottle- necks.

However, the security threats as discussed above, commonly characterized by political strife, organized criminal activities, and terrorism, religious extremism and human security concerns, which complicate the architecture of any international cooperation for peace. Response and interventions by international actors, particularly in intra state conflict situation may require a regional approach in the containment, management and resolution of these conflicts. Regional organizations and agencies therefore are key actors in international politics, in particular in the maintenance of peace and security of the region.[33] Therefore, any international response takes into account the significance of regional organization in addressing peace and security issues.

National and Regional Responses and Strategies

States and regional communities in East Africa are constantly devising strategies and policies to deal with the security concerns that the region is grappling with. The region is witnessing positive transformations and is emerging as a security community, which is characterized by mutual sympathy and loyalties; of 'we-feeling,' trust, and mutual consideration; of partial identification in terms of self-images and interests. The key indicators are shared identities, values, and meanings; many-sided direct interactions, and reciprocal long-term interest, which is evident in East Africa Community. The free movement of investments, goods and services across the five states that make up the East African Community, the emergence of multi party politics, the progress in democratization process and the development of a shared identity are all indications of a security community that is slowly but surely emerging in the region.

Regionally, the strategies that have been adopted goes a long way in enhancing the East African Community spirit of co-operation in regional peace and security, which brings into reality the collective responsibility in provision of security by the Partner States. It covers collaboration on cross border crimes, auto theft, drug trafficking, terrorism, money laundering and other crimes

International responses and cooperation

While states and region are making efforts towards mitigating security risks for securing a peaceful and stable environment, it is also realized that the security threats that the region is facing are such that it cannot be only addressed at the national and regional level. Majority of the wars and armed conflicts in East Africa have been described as complex political emergencies, which requires a combination of efforts. Exploring possibilities for partnership is therefore useful in tackling the challenges in East Africa.

There is a need for international cooperation for responding to the changing nature of peace and security. The widespread impact of terrorism for example, increases gravity of such threats which require extraordinary measures such as combining security efforts through regional or international partnerships. The most recent threats to human security perhaps reflect the direction global peace and security is taking. For example, the cause and effect relationship between conventional security and human security gives rise to symptoms such as religious and ideological conflicts, ethnicity, economic conflicts, and energy supplies as well as the actions of state and non-state actors.

The magnitude of these conflicts requires international cooperation or intervention, even though the regional organizations are increasingly playing a responsible role in responding to these challenges. In terms of logistics, capacity building, intelligence sharing, technology and techniques, international partnership becomes significant in order to respond effectively to the complex challenges. On their part, the international actors response to the security challenges is determined not only by their commitment to global peace and security, but also by their economic and security interest.

The international actors have faced the challenge of having to respond by managing the situation, supporting recovery activities as well as putting structures in place to prevent escalation of conflicts. The responses had gone beyond the mandate or capacity of any single agency or the UN. It often took the form of humanitarian relief, security and military operations and a range of nation-building interventional programmes.

Though the regional bodies play the primary role in addressing the security concerns in the region, the role of international actors also assumes immense significance given the complexity of the challenges.

Areas of Security Cooperation between India and East Africa

India on its part has been contributing to the peace and security efforts in the region according to its capacity and capability. However, for resolving the complex security challenges, efforts towards building long-term coalition of East African states and India are essential towards the delivery of effective and efficient peace operations. This co-operative arrangement would create the conditions for broadening peace efforts other than peacekeeping, including political diplomatic and socio-economic dimensions. Some of the areas where India is cooperating with East Africa countries for ensuring peace and stability are maritime security, anti-piracy and anti –terrorism, capacity building, doctrines and best practices and research, which are discussed in greater detail below. These areas of security cooperation need greater focus from both sides.

Maritime Security: Combating Piracy

The eastern seaboard of Africa falls under India's strategic neighbourhood, as 90 percent of India's oil import transit through the Gulf of Aden. But piracy in Somalia waters has been a threat to international shipping and commercial seaborne trade including that of India. From the period 2008-2011 about 95 percent of the piracy in international waters was done by Somali pirates. The area had overtaken the Straits of Malacca in Southeast Asia. Moreover it is an organized industry with pirates acquiring new levels of confidence where they try to negotiate prisoner exchange. The incident where the pirates decided to retain seven Indian sailors as hostages after releasing the ship and receiving the full ransom from its Mumbai-based owner, in order to negotiate the release of 120 Somali pirates held in Indian jails is a case in point. Analysts say that such assertiveness on the part of pirates could be a result of the encouragement they get from terrorist groups. There are fears that the ungoverned territories of Somalia could become a terrorist state financed by pirate revenues. This further raises concerns about the security of the Indian Ocean region.

As far as India is concerned India has a strong interest in ensuring the security of maritime traffic as piracy incurs a tremendous cost on India's maritime trade and threatens its prospects as a trading superpower. India's trade that passes through the Gulf of Aden estimated at about 110 billion dollars annually. About 24 Indian flagged merchant ships transit the Gulf of Aden every month. Moreover, more than six percent of seafarers engaged in international shipping companies are Indian nationals. The responses to deal with the threat of piracy in Somalia waters so far have been military and police action. India on its part has been maintaining a naval presence since 2008 in the piracy prone areas in the Gulf of Aden and has been rendering assistance to merchant ships irrespective of the nationality. Besides naval presence India had also proposed a five point plan to the UN Security Council to tackle the problem of piracy off the coast of Somalia which includes the following (i) Reinforcement of tracking the trail of ransom money to different parts of the world as entrusted to the Interpol; (ii) Prosecution of the beneficiaries of ransom money for abetting piracy; (iii) Consideration of the conduct of the naval operations under the UN as the preferred option; (iv) Sanitisation of the Somali coast line through identified corridors and buffer zones and tracking of fishing vessels around the Somali coast and (v)Enactment of national laws on priority to criminalize piracy as defined in the UN Convention on the Law of the Sea and the prosecution of suspected, and imprisonment of convicted, pirates apprehended off the coast of Somalia as required under resolution 1918 (2010). The five point plan although is a positive step, yet it would require larger time frame to execute it. Moreover to curb piracy these measures would not be sufficient.

A land based strategy is very important to deal with this growing organized industry of piracy. So far defensive and containment strategy in the high seas adopted by India along with others has been limited and has a short-term impact. The UN Security Council resolution 1851 adopted on 16 Dec 2008 authorizes land-based operations in Somalia by laying down that States and regional organizations could undertake all necessary measures" appropriate in Somalia", to interdict those using Somali territory to plan, facilitate or undertake such acts (of piracy). However despite this mandate there has been limited action to deal with the problem on land. It could be because of lack of national and collective will or could be because lack of interest on the place itself. It also could be for the fact that the nations in Africa do not want to overstretch themselves. Such an exercise would be costly and require commitment of troops. Importantly for India, given its huge strategic interest in the Gulf of Aden, it is essential to partner with African nations in general and East African countries in particular, which have immediate stakes in the region to deal with this menace.

In this context India's call to the African nations in the II Africa- India Forum Summit at Addis Ababa to jointly combat piracy and a pledge for contributing $2 million for the AU mission in Somalia stands significant. While continuing with the military action India needs to partner both bilaterally with countries having stake in Somalia, particularly with East African countries such as Ethiopia, Kenya, Tanzania and also multilaterally with AU. Meanwhile the Indian navy now regularly patrols the Somali waters as well in the Western Indian Ocean region for anti-piracy assistance which has led to drop in piracy attacks in the Indian Ocean.

Besides piracy the Indian navy was also quietly deployed in early January 2008 during the height of the post-election political crisis in Kenya in case the situation deteriorated to the point that evacuation of Kenyan NRIs was necessary. The Indian government had announced that urgent visas could be issued to needy individuals. With memories of India's failure to intervene in support of East African Asians in 1968 and 1971 from Kenya and 1972 from Uganda, the Indian navy wanted to be ready in case it became politically expeditious to engage in a civilian evacuation mission, as it did in Beirut in 2006 with the assistance of four Indian navy ships. It is interesting to note the extent to which the projection of Indian naval capacity globally resonates with nationalist sentiments within the country.

The Indian navy is also part of maritime military block comprising of littoral states of the Indian Ocean, known as the Indian Ocean Naval Symposium (IONS). This includes 33 countries ranging from South Africa to Australia and would not exclude Pakistan (although China and the US have been excluded thus far). According to Indian officials the IONS aims to 'increase maritime cooperation among participating navies/maritime agencies by providing a forum for discussion of maritime issues, both global and regional, and in the process generate a flow of information and opinion between naval professionals leading to common understanding and possible agreements on the way ahead'[34] . The IONS is also a response to the fact that, although India is a member of the nine-nation South Asia Regional Port Security Cooperative, maritime issues are not adequately covered by this body or within the IOR-ARC, although India is looking at how it might revive the IOR-ARC under its presidency in 2011.

Convergence and potential for Cooperation on Counter terrorism

EAC states and India have been victim of terrorism, particularly religious terrorism. Both have common push factors of poverty and unemployment amongst the youth that makes them vulnerable for recruitment, indoctrination and radicalization by terrorist elements. The youth who account for the bulk of the population in the two cases are the main perpetrators of terror activities. There is a need to adequately address the twin issues of poverty and unemployment of youth who will continue to provide support for terror activities.

In both cases terrorism having religious connotation, have perpetrators coming predominantly from the Muslim faith disguised under the banner of a *jihad*. In both cases however there are sizable populations of the Muslim faith who are law abiding and do not subscribe to terrorist ideals. In both instances counter terrorism strategies have been misinterpreted as discriminatory or targeting the Muslim faith. This perception frustrates any efforts towards counter terrorism legislation. There is also a tremendous rise in religious fundamentalism that is propagating the ideology of *Jihad (holy* war) and *Fidayeen* (suicide attacks).

In both cases terrorism has been internationalized, with most support, funding, training, logistics and planning having a foreign element, with Pakistan featuring as a source for both. Both have challenges in border control and management, making it easy for terrorists to freely move in and out of their territories. In both the criminal elements can easily get safe havens with homogenous religious communities from where they can operate without much difficulty or detection.

The strategies being implemented in are to a certain extent similar and include deterrence, legislation, disruption, enhancing border controls and surveillance, policing, criminal administration and establishment of multi-agency centres where security and other concerned agencies conduct their operations. The strategies adopted in both have made some modest progress in deterring terror attacks, but their inherent weaknesses still need to be addressed. These weaknesses include the ineffective — or lack of — counter-terrorism legislation, reactive responses and slow government decision making, lack of clear strategies and policies regarding terrorism, and the structural inadequacies of the state apparatus in the respective countries. Both are considered American/western allies, makes them key targets for international terror groups like the *Al Qaeda,* who see them as proxies to attack American or western interests in their respective countries. Terrorism will remain an issue of concern to both EAC states and India. There are however opportunities to work together to be able to address some elements of the threat more specifically those which are common to both.

Capacity Building partnership

Capacity Building is another potential area of cooperation that could be exploited in order to contribute to enhancement of peace operations capability in East Africa. First, technical assistance in infrastructural development is one of the vehicles India uses to build cooperation with African countries. The opportunities in this approach lies in the weak infrastructural status of countries in the continent. For example, efforts by Kenya, Uganda and Tanzania to maintain efficient railway line have always been mired by technical and financial constraint. Yet, a robust railway system would not only serve to reduce social distance with India but also act as a means of ensuring effective surveillance of the fragile East African coastal region against the activities of the pirates and other organized crimes.

Second, a review of the Rapid Deployment Capability (RDC) of the ASF indicated inadequate capability to respond within 14 days. Apparently any form of peace operation is dependent on UN support. Yet, the 2003 ASF Framework Policy encourages AU to cooperate not only with the UN but also other international actors to deploy in circumstances of emergency. Moreover, best practices within the UN provide for options of conducting capacity-building initiatives such as training and exercises. These initiatives may require multilateral arrangements where Indian expertise and experience stands relevant.

Moreover, it is clear that the African Peace Fund (APF) covers African countries' military deployment in Africa, but does not cover ammunitions, arms and specific military equipments, salaries for troops and military training for soldiers. The latter activities are critical capacity-building initiatives that would require external support for filling the resource gap. The UN experience in African regions such as Darfur indicates that the host communities in conflict zones tend to reject non-African troops in their territories and this could escalate conflict. While multilateral arrangements could encompass majority of actors, including the UN, India with her long history in Eastern Africa may serve to mitigate this situation.

The relation between India and the rest of Africa is obviously driven by several factors. One of the factors borders on human security in the continuous supply of food, energy and trade deals. It is therefore most likely that India would broaden the interests to cover peace and security. East Africa will have to significantly tap from India's robust navy for joint operations in the Indian Ocean to curb the pirate menace. For the case of Tanzania and Kenya, without strong Indian Ocean surveillance the menace of piracy may persist, the situation could easily be arrested through collaborative initiatives to tap from the mighty India's Navy.

To fulfill the task of developing long-term peacekeeping capability for the East Africa sub-region through the Eastern African Standby Force (EASF), peacekeeping training centres would be instrumental in initiating exchange programmes for military personnel. In this vein, a possibility of attachments amongst the military personnel of the cooperating partners is germane. Peacekeeping institutions in the sub-region such as the IPSTC, government establishments such as the DSC and NDC as well as the sub-regional standby force (EASF) could form the basis for this collaboration. At the same time the standardization of the training and exercises of the partner institutions is key to the success of joint peace operations.

In respect to the peacekeeping personnel capacity-building, the cooperation between India and East African sub-region could be utilized in supporting establishment of a training facility in post-war Somalia. Fragility of a post-war state is characterized by several weaknesses including lack of military training facilities and lack of skilled personnel for supporting peace operations. In pursuit of this goal, peace and security actors in the sub-region will have to utilize the already existing training facilities and extent such services to Somalia as part of the operational strategy for post-conflict reconstruction and development. But, establishment of a peacekeeping training facility requires capital investment. It should be noted that Kenya, Uganda, Burundi, and Ethiopia are taking lead in neutralizing the activities of the Al Shabaab group in Somalia under the helm of AMISOM. This implies that almost the entire sub-region will be instrumental in rebuilding post-war Somalia. Given this scenario, it is obvious that these states will shoulder the burden of mobilizing the required resources for peace support operation (PSO) in the Horn of Africa. In this case therefore, India will have to significantly explore possibilities of engaging the sub-region in a multifaceted fashion. Chances are India will be comfortable extending hand through diplomatic commerce and peacekeeping enablement arrangements such as equipments and skill transfer.

Also, the historical ties between India and East Africa and the economic adventure by the Indian community could as well as serve as a model for the development of cooperation in fields beyond economic investment such as peace operations. For this to be fulfilled there is need coordination of efforts by establishing focal points in each of the cooperating countries.

To benefit from the established focal points which can be instrumental in the creation of backward-forward linkages, relevant government sectors such as defence and internal security guidance is necessary. Even though collaboration could be handled by various units and international forums, absence of government sectors would delay partnership agreements. It is notable that currently the government sectors such as the defence impresses multilateral cooperation. The International Peace Support Training Centre (IPSTC) through its peacekeeping training and research programmes serves as an example of efforts by the sub-regional peace and security actors towards building platforms for international cooperation.

Furthermore, India's Technical and Economic Cooperation (ITEC) would serve as a platform for exchange of programmes for strengthening peace support operations (PSOs). A close collaboration with peacekeeping Centres of Excellence in Eastern Africa such as the International Peace Support Training Centre (IPSTC) in Nairobi would be most welcome. Moreover co-operative arrangement can create the conditions for broadening peace efforts other than peacekeeping, including political and diplomatic dimensions.

The process of building capability could be described as capital investment that may require combination of efforts in form of partnerships. Perhaps, India with its international experience in peacekeeping including on the United Nations Mission in Sierra Leone (UNAMSIL) and the UN Mission between Ethiopia and Eritrea (UNMEE) serves as a gateway for a partnership with East Africa. Furthermore, the contribution of India in training the South African National Defence Force (SANDF) for peacekeeping missions depicts the sub-continent as an extraordinary force and its commitment to the international peace and stability.[35] Indeed, India has previously invested in future African military leaders by training thousands of Officers from a number of African countries in the academies of its three service branches as well as the postgraduate National Defence College in New Delhi and Defence Services Staff College in Wellington. The peace operation training centres in East Africa including the International

Peace Support Training Centre(IPSTC) in Nairobi could serve to strengthen this opportunities for mutual benefit of the cooperating partners(CoP) not only for training military personnel but also civilian and the police in courses such as security sector reforms(SSR), rule of law(RoL) and disaster management.

Sharing of Best Practices

The first step in building co-operative frameworks is the establishment of clear operating standards. The definition of core operational standards assists in the design of effective basic training and pre-deployment preparations. These standards must be based on real situations and tasks experienced on the ground by troop contributing countries. Challenges related to co-operation for peace operations in East Africa are multiple. One of them is the variety of peace actors and their approach to the problem. Thus, while seeking to achieve the objective of sustainable peace, peace-building and development activities, the divergent cultures and relationships must be harmonized. Hence, scholars and practitioners need 'ongoing conversations across the co-operating partner's cultural divide' to achieve a basic consensus on the shape of the peace to be built.

India has a rich experience in peacekeeping and a remarkable record of effectiveness on the ground. Beyond the undisputable quality of the peacekeepers themselves and their leadership, one factor noted on many occasions is the ability of the Indian contingents to adjust to local conditions and to 'blend-in' the local environment, while providing an added value to the local population. An example is South Sudan, where the Indian contingent deployed in Malakal used simple traditional Indian technology to build their camp using readily available and environment friendly resources. Engineers of the contingent also realised that this technology could be shared with the local population to build more durable and comfortable houses, and they organized training courses. This initiative was welcomed by the local authorities as it improved the life of the local population in a sustainable way. This is the kind of best practices and lessons that could be shared in such exchanges. Unfortunately, lessons learned processes tend to remain confined to national establishments and best practices to remain unknown to other actors. While it is true that some lessons learned address internal issues that cannot be shared with others, there is a wealth of best practices that can be shared.

Research priority concerns

There is a need for collaborative efforts in operational research and analysis in all the domains of peace operations. This would identify relevant aspects of modern and complex conflicts for capability development. The improvement of training capabilities through enhanced use of simulation could also be a rich area for operational research with opportunities for measurable results. Modeling standard exercises and its multiple variants can be an area of fruitful co-operation between India and East African countries, where capabilities of India in software development have been recognized worldwide in the last decades.

Research and simulation do not only enhance the quality of training, but also reduce the environmental footprint of peacekeeping and improve its cost effectiveness ratio. As such they provide new exploration fields for possible co-operation. For instance, the United Service Institution of India (USI) hosts, together with the Centre for Strategic Studies and Simulation (CSS) and covers similar functionalities to the IPSTC in Nairobi. Both institutions could benefit from their mutual experience in peacekeeping in East Africa through collaborative research and modeling projects

Post-conflict Recovery

The issue of reconstruction and restoration of order requires a careful approach. India's experience and expertise in addressing local issues without disrupting a system would be essential in the context of post conflict recovery situation in Africa. India could significantly explore the possibilities of engaging the sub-region in a multifaceted fashion. Chances are that India would be comfortable in collaborating through diplomatic, economic and peacekeeping capability arrangements such as equipment and skills transfer. The Indian community's economic success in conjunction with already existing historical relations with East Africa could serve as a model for the development of co-operation in fields beyond economic investment such as peace operations. Inter-organizational collaboration is key to the fight against trans-boundary violence by way of pooling resources and harmonizing tasks and mandates. Currently many international arrangements and organizations prefer multilateral regimes not only because of the globalisation of security threats and the rising demand for peace operations, but also because it provides legitimacy. However while the achievement of efficiency in peace operations can be linked to availability of certain capabilities such as logistics and command structures, efficiency could also be significantly influenced by the complexity of peace operations specific to regions.

Collaboration Strategic efforts

The effectiveness and efficiency of peace operations is a function of advanced operational capabilities. These capabilities are invaluable in meeting the challenges of complex peace missions characterized by, regional conflict dynamics, and extremist groups like *Al-Shabaab*. An example of a mission that to some extent seeks to facilitate the extension of state authority through peacekeeping is the case for Somalia and its protracted conflict.

African states contribute nearly 60,000 troops through the UN, AU and other organisations reflecting a major commitment by Africa to find solutions to African problems. However, African contributions suffer from the inability of the majority of troop contributing countries to match this level of personnel to the supply of force enablers and multipliers such as engineering units and helicopters.

Based on these considerations, it is clearly necessary to find ways to better exploit the experience available on both sides of the Indian Ocean to generate better and more efficient training, and new and more consensual ideas about how new forms of conflicts should be approached. This requires regular and even institutionalized exchanges of information on best practices and conflict analyses to improve conflict prevention, conflict management and post-conflict recovery

Conclusion

Based on the analysis in the paper, it is plausible to argue that the current structural and political challenges facing peace and security in the East Africa will require a collective approach. Subsequently, due to the complex peace and security environment prevailing in the sub-region, external support is indispensable. The chapter has shown that whether bilaterally or through multilateral arrangements there are several opportunities that India and the sub-region could engage in to support the peace and stability in the region. Though India and East African states enjoy warm relation at diplomatic level, solid cooperation structures will require to be instituted.

End Notes

1   EmmaMawdsley, Gerard tc, Cann (ed), India in Africa: Changing Geographies of power, Fahamu Books

2   India Defence, 2008Indian Navy to hold excercises with France, African Navies, 17 August

3   Lemarchand, (1997), Patterns of State Collapse and Reconstruction in Central Africa: Reflections on Crisis in the Great Lakes Regio', *Africa Spectrum*, Vol.32, No.2

4   Bratton, (2004), 'State Building and Democratiza Sub-Saharan Africa: Forward, Backward or Together', *4frobarotneter Working paper*, No. 43

5   Khadiagala (2003), Burundi: In Dealing with Conflicts in Africa: The United Nations and Regional organizations, ed. J Boulden , New York: Palgrave Macmillan

6   Damari Nyaboke Manyange,Converging Interests in East Africa-India Security Relations: Lessons from Counter Terrorism Strategies, Makumi Mwagiru (ed) East Africa-India Security Relations

7   ibid

8   Shinn, D, (2003), 'terrorism in East Africa and the Horn of Africa: An Overview', *Journal of Conflict Studies*, Fall (20)

9   Damari Nyaboke Manyange,Converging Interests in East AAfrica-India Security Relations: Lessons from Counter Terrorism Strategies ,Makumi Mwagiru (ed) East Africa-India Security Relations

10   ibid

11   Okuma, W & Botha, A (ed) (2007), Understanding Terrorism in Africa: Building bridges and Overcoming gaps, Institute of Security Studies

12   ibid

13   Mutiga Mrithi, (2004) How the Terrorist Attack was planned and Executed , East African Standard, (Nairobi0,November 27, 2004.

14   Baulch B. (ed (2010), Why Poverty Persisits:Poverty Dynam,icsin Asiaand Africa,Cheltenham:Edward Edger.

15   Suri *et al,* (2008)Poverty, Inequalitynad Income Dynamics in Kenya, 1997-2007, Nairobi: Tegemeo Institute, Working paper Seeries, 30/2008

16   Mwambu,et al   (2005),Review of Policy optionsfor Poverty Reduction in Kenya, Nairobi,KIPPRA, Discussion paper No 49

17   Kiwanuka, G, (2003),Malaria Morbidity and Mortality in Uganda'< Journal of Vector Borne Diseases, June

18   Singh S (2005/2006), Food Security-Effectivenessof the Public Distribution System in india, Ljbubljana University, MBA Thesis (unpublished)

19   Taylor D B, et al (2011) Nutrition in Central Uganda: An estimation of a Minimum Healthy Diet', http://ageconsearch.umn.edu/bitstream/103603/2/Badirwand, percent20Nakakeeto, percent20Rudi, percent20Taylor.pdf

20   Njuki Mwaniki,(2012),State and Human Security in East Africs: Lessons from India's Experience, (ed) Makumi Mwagiru and Aparajita Biswas, East Africa –India Security Relations

21   Klopp. J 2008,Kenya's Unfinished Agenda's, International Affairs, Vol 62,no 2

22   Reuters, 2011

23   Jackson, (2009).,Violent Conflicts and the African States: Towards a Framework of Analysis', Journal of Contemporary African Studies,20(1),pp 29-52

24   Akwambai D and Ateyo P.E, ,(2007),The Scramble for Cattle, Power and Guns in Karamoja,BostonFeinstein international centre, Tufts university

25   Lemacharnd, 1997R. (10997(, 'patterns of Statte collapse and Reconstruction in Central Africa: Reflections on Crisis in the Great Lakes Region', African Spectrum, Vol 32, no 2

26   Musambayi Katumanga, (2012) Closed Spaces and Geo Politicsin the Pivot Triangle: Perspectives for Emerging Asian Powers,in Makumi Mwagiru and aparajita Biswas (ed) East Africa- India Security Relations

27   See Keen, D. (2008). Complex Emergencies.

28   See The African Peace and Security Architecture (APSA): 2010 Assessment Study. - Source of information courtesy of the first ordinary session of the Assembly of the African Union in Durban, South Africa, on 9 July 2002 and

entered into force on 23 December 2003. - Source of information courtesy of the second extraordinary session of the Assembly of Heads of State and Government of the AU, held in Sirte, Lybia, on 27-28 FeB. 2004 Source of information courtesy of Carten Stahn, Responsibility to protect: political rhetoric or emerging legal norm? American Journal of International law. 101(2007), 99, 100-101. See The African Development Bank: East African Integration Strategy 2011-2015. See The African Development Bank: African Development Fund: Eastern Africa, Regional integration strategy paper, 2011-2015. Regional Development-OREA/OREB, October, 2010

29 Macharia Munene (2012) *Historical Reflections on Kenya: Intellectual Adventurism, Politics & International Relations* University of Nairobi Press

30 See Francis, D.J. (2001). The Politics of Economic Regionalism. See Buzan, B. & Weaver. (2003). Regions and Powers.

31 Ibid.

32 See The European Commission, Securing peace and stability for Africa: The EU-Funded African Peace Facility. Brussels: European Commission, July 2004.

33 See Francis, D.J. (2007). Uniting Africa: Building regional peace and security systems, Ashgate. University of Bradford, UK.

34 Financial Express, Indian Navy Floats maritime military Block, 8 February 2008

35 See Xenia, D.(2007). Is India, or Will It Be, a Responsible International Stakeholder? Washington Quarterly, Vol. 30, No. 3: 117-130. See Pham, J.P. (2006). The Sierra Leon Tragedy: History and Global dimensions; New York, 148-151. See Griffin, C. (2006). What India wants, Armed Forces Journal, Vol. 143, No. 10: 16-18.

Conclusions

The India- East Africa relationship has existed for a long time now. It predates the birth of the East African states and India. Over the years the relations has witnessed various changes. It has moved from a period of high political and moral solidarity to a more material, concrete and pragmatic approach. Particularly after the 2008 India- Africa Forum Summit, it has seen a renewed vigour. The contemporary partnership reckons into account winds of change in their respective territories and the emerging realities of the globalised world. It takes into account their changed status in the international system. India's rise as an economic power and a key global player and East Africa's growth, quietly purposeful and incremental are shaping the character and complexion of the evolving relationship. Their change in status has changed their priorities and imperatives. Based on striking complementarities between both sides, new areas of cooperation have emerged providing opportunities for deeper engagement. The model of engagement is partnership based, which India claims to be different from others, as it is request based and is one seeking mutual benefit through a consultative process. The cooperation centers on trade, private sector investment, development assistance and capacity building, security and diaspora. This book focused on these areas of cooperation wherein it examined the opportunities and concerns.

Development partnership programmes have strengthened India-East Africa relations. Since long, India has been contributing to East Africa's development. But recently, particularly after the 2008 India-Africa Summit, India has been in limelight for its enhanced involvement in East Africa's development process, through various initiatives. The development initiatives and programmes are linked to its strengths and foreign policy objectives. But it is different from the traditional donors as well as other emerging powers. From a recipients' perspective it provides comparative advantage. The India Development Initiative effort is a tool to strengthen south-south cooperation and support the national efforts of East African countries while promoting India's long-term interests.

India's development assistance, however, is still small in terms of funds transferred, but it is not insignificant. It may create a new platform for South-South dialogue and it is framed as a partnership between equal partners, which may enhance the developmental aspect of it. Moreover, it tends to focus on trade-related issues. It is a combination of tied project aid and scholarships; a large part of what India spends is on development assistance in human resource development and capacity building. India is increasingly aware of the need to improve the material standards of East African people in order that the continent's global economic leverage is increased. India has wealth of experiences in various sectors which it believes in sharing with the East African countries for their growth and development. This development cooperation is done at bilateral as well as multilateral level. It is implemented by various ministries and institutions such as EXIM bank, with the Ministry of External Affairs (MEA) as the leading ministry. East African countries which have a strong Indian presence have been beneficiaries of this programmes and initiatives; both bilaterally and regionally. During the two Africa-Indian Summits Africa and India laid the foundations for a stronger development-centric partnership revolving around capacity building, HRD, training and trade.

India's development cooperation policy approach is clearly distinct from the OECD/DAC approach, the principles of non-interference and mutual respect for sovereignty remaining major features. India's engagement with development partners is different in motivation, intent and history from that of the Western aid givers, without any conditionalities.

Besides the expected benefits from India's development cooperation for East African countries, there also remain some challenges and risks. India's development efforts have been compared with China, which need not be done, since both countries have different ideologies, resources and strengths. They also have distinct and divergent reasons to follow different approaches delivering and harnessing development, primarily safeguarding their interests. While compared to China and other traditional donors India cannot match their grant-in-aid, it is moving to become a major strategic player in development assistance, and its foot print is slowly becoming prominent. What India should be cautious about is to balance its interest with those of its East African assistance partners, otherwise there is a danger of sacrificing the goodwill which it has earned over the years. For this an effective monitoring and evaluation mechanism and transparency of its development assistance programmes must be maintained.

The East African countries including Tanzania and Uganda have been beneficiaries of capacity building programmes, like ITEC and the Indian Council for Cultural Relations (ICCR) Scholarship Programme. However expectations are still high from India with regard to assistance for human resource development. Scholarships are considered to be limited in scope, as far as developing human capital is concerned. Expectations are for Indian faculty teaching in their Universities. For instance Uganda prefers Indian faculty to teach at Uganda Management Institute rather than setting up Institute (IIFT) like Indian Institute of Foreign Trade, as laid down in India- Africa Summit declaration. In Tanzania the Institute of Finance Management and IIFT have a collaboration where Indian faculty go and teach there. So what India needs to factor is the needs and requirements of the East African countries while formulating plans and programmes for development and growth in East Africa.

In the context of trade and investment between India and East African countries there are immense opportunities. Indian entrepreneurs are very keen regarding opportunities in East Africa. According to Ministry of Finance of India, the country's approved cumulative investment in East Africa from April 1996 to October 2010 amounted to USS 186.67 million.. Kenya with a total investment of $149.4 million was the top destination of India's overseas direct investments (ODI) in the East Africa region. Investments and cooperation in sectors like agriculture, health, information and communication technology (ICT), education, capacity building, and skills transfer have been the backbone of India's partnership with East Africa.

EAC's total trade with India stood at more than USD 3.3 billion in 2010 which was 8.27 per cent of India's total trade with Africa. The share of EAC's trade in India's total trade with Africa over past 5 years has increased from 5.07 per cent to 7.97 per cent. An analysis of the bilateral trade between India and each of the EAC member countries reveals that Kenya leads the group followed by Tanzania and Uganda. India is the biggest exporter of pharmaceutical products to the EAC region. Its key competitors in this category are Denmark, Kenya, Belgium and Switzerland but they lag far behind India. The slowdown of the developed economies and the consequent drying up of aid and foreign capital flows to the East African Community region present both challenges and opportunities for Indian companies. With a long term business strategy, India could benefit from economic partnership with the East African Community region. Indian investments are not only improving farm technologies and productivity in East Africa. They are also promoting agro-business through technical assistance and skills transfers. This is an area with good scope for.

However, the economic relation that emerged in the context of Indian initiatives in the umbrella of South-South was not very equitable at least on trade. Indo-East African growing trends in economic areas demand that in the light of India's past experiences, it should be sensitive to East African concerns and expectations. If the growing trends under Indian private sectors in Indo-East African economic relations do not distinguish it qualitatively from North-South relations, then it would create problems for Indian moves in Africa. The economic relations of India with East Africa under globalisation are gainful for India but it has to be qualitatively different from North-South relations as far as African perceptions are concerned.

Diaspora remains another crucial factor in India- East Africa current engagement, which provides opportunities to strengthen the relations. Over the years the Indians in East African countries have attained affluence in the economic field but in the political field their role has been marginal. Among the Indians in these three countries the socio-political situation of Indians in Kenya and Tanzania was better than Uganda, which is due to moderate policies put forth by the respective government that provided them with opportunities to flourish in the political and economic sphere. In Uganda they have faced worst crisis. However, with President Yoweri Museveni coming to power they were integrated as 54th tribe in the constitution.

The Indian government, however, has not really focused on the Indians in East Africa which is why many of the big Indian business groups of Indian origin in that continent do not look at putting their money in India but instead tap business opportunities in Europe and America. However, if certain restrictions were eased and some steps are taken by the government, India could attract a lot of investment from this segment. Besides it could harness the vast knowledge and experience of the Indian business community in East Africa. Especially the local ground knowledge of companies could be tapped by Indian players looking at partnerships in the region.

There are many Indian business groups operating in East African countries. The big business houses from India such as the Tatas, Essar, Vedanta, and Kirloskar who are now operating in East Africa are in many cases engaged with the Indian diaspora there, including talented professionals of Indian origin. But somehow the broader links are not yet being built and there seems to be a lack of policy level engagement by the Indian government particularly taking into account the uniqueness of this diaspora in East Africa. Prominent members of the Indian business community in Africa feel that there's not enough being done on the part of the Indian government to engage with them, even as India reaches out to people of Indian origin in the West in a much bigger way. India therefore needs to recognize this diaspora as a strategic heritage resource in order to have a strong engagement.

The Indians are economically well integrated in East African countries. Any economic analysis of India- East Africa relations cannot ignore the Indian Diaspora. However, the relevance of the diaspora in defining economic ties might get limited in the future. Indians investing in East Africa are not much associating themselves with Indian Africans. Indian businesses are not necessarily looking for partners of Indian descent on the continent. They are just looking for good business partners. The companies from East African countries like Tanzania, which are now investing in India, are primarily owned by PIOs not the locals. According to the locals the Indian community (PIO) is not socially integrated as the Chinese. They feel Chinese do not have the advantage like Indians with regard to networks, lobbying, language and culture yet they are good at doing business.

On the aspect of security, it is observed that the region is fraught with various threats ranging from non-traditional securities such as threat of piracy, religious terrorism, rise of Islamic forces, insecurity in the Indian Ocean, human security related to poverty and deprivation, and food security is plausible to argue that such security challenges facing threatening peace and security in the East Africa will require a collective approach. Subsequently, due to the complex peace and security environment prevailing in the sub-region, external support is indispensable. Whether bilaterally or through multilateral arrangements there are several opportunities that India and the sub-region could engage in to support the ongoing peace operations efforts in the East Africa. India could try and partner in the proposed multilateral and regional counter-terror initiatives in East Africa.

India also needs to articulate its position on political and security crisis situations in East Africa more proactively and in pronounced fashion.

Though India and East African states enjoy warm relation at diplomatic level, solid cooperation structures will require to be instituted. India should be able to harmonize its South–South coordination policy and its interests in order to have a sustainable long term partnership. Business and governments need to strike deals that not only generate wealth but help eradicate poverty by investing in East Africa's peoples. The strategic partnership between India and East Africa should bring tangible solutions for various issues which are included in the African Programme namely NEPAD (The New Partnership for Africa's Development).Particularly expansion of development of infrastructure facilities which will enhance facilitate intra East African trade and economic development in the continent and facilitate trade, economic co-operation and provide improved market access for East African products.

As far as visibility in terms of development deliverables of India in East Africa are concerned still much needs to be done. India needs to expand its presence and pay greater attention to implementation of the projects. For ensuring an effective implementation of development projects, regular monitoring and timely review are required. There is also the need to address the structural deficiency of the IAFS process, which is premised on the Banjul formula, giving primacy to discretion and decision of the AU Commission, rather than considering the choice and judgement of the concerned country, where the development projects are being implemented. India needs to see that the initiatives and partnership programmes not only benefits it, but also suits the requirements and needs of local people. For the sustenance and consolidation of the rising India-East Africa cooperation a multi-stakeholder approach and social auditing is necessary. Due consideration needs to be given to what things can be done jointly to promote the growth of the relationship. Specific policy needs to be designed for engaging Indian diaspora in East Africa, keeping in view their uniqueness, in terms of heterogeneity, social positioning and complex identity. The policy announcement of partnership on harnessing diaspora in the 2008 IAFS declaration for mutual benefits calls for priority attention in the case of East Africa. Finally the perceptions and needs of both sides require to match otherwise they will become stumbling block for prosperity.

Bibliography

Africa Economic Outlook, Burundi, 2012

African Union Commission, 2006, 'Draft Report of the Meeting of the Task Force in Africa's Strategic Partnership with Emerging Powers: China, India and Brazil', Addis Ababa.

Al-Masudi, 'The Ivory Trade', G.S.P Freeman Grenville, pp 14-15

Alden,C. 2005 'Leveraging the Dragon: toward an Africa that can Say', *Jo- e Africa - Electronic Journal of Governance and Innovation*, February.

Alden,C. and Alves, A.C. 'China's Africa policy', *Review of African Political Economy*, vol. 35, no. 115, p. 43

Alden,C. 2008 'An Africa without Europeans', in Alden,C, Large,D and Soares de Oliviera, R. (eds) *China Returns to Africa: A Superpower and a Continent Embrace*, London, Hurst.

Anderson David M. 2010, 'The Politics of Oil in Eastern Africa', IAAMS Lecture delivered at the International Alumni Association of Scoula Mattci at Geneva, 15 October.

Ayoob, M. 1995, *The Third World Security Predicament: State Making, Regional Conflict and the International System*, Boulder, Lynne Rienner Publishers, London.

Bachmann,V. 2011, 'European Spaces of Development: Aid, Regulation and Regional Integration' in: Bialasiewicz L. (ed) *Europe in the World: EU Geopolitics and the Themes of nation of European Space*, Aldershot, Ashgate, pp 59-84

Bajpaee, C. 2008, 'The Indian elephant returns to Africa', Online Asia Times, 25 April http://www.atimes.com/atimes.

Bayart, J.F. 1993, *The State in Africa: The Politics of the Belly*, London, Longman.

Ben Macintyre, 2010, 'The Battle Against Piracy Begins in Mogadishu,' TIMESONLINE, April 1; Garowe Online, "Somalia: Amison Denies Al-Shabaub Claims", http://allafrica.com/stories/printable/20 I 002120931.html.

Bhaskar, C.Uday & Kemp Geoffrey. 2011, 'Maritime Security Challenges in the Indian Ocean Region', A Workshop Report, New Delhi

Bhattacharya Sanjukta, 2010, 'Engaging Africa: India's interest in the African continent, Past and Present', in Cheru, F. and Obi, C. (eds) *The Rise of China and India in Africa*, London and Uppsala, Zed Books and The Nordic Africa Institute.

Bharti, A. 1972, *Asians in East Africa: Jayhind and Uhuru*, Nelson Hall, Chicago,pp. 175-76.

Biswas, Aparajita. 2012 'Changing Perspectives of Indian Perspectives of Indian Engagements in Africa', *Indian Foreign affairs Journal*, Vol 7, no 1.

Bratton, 2004, 'State Building and Democratization in Sub-SaharanAfrica: Forward, Backward or Together', Afrobarometer Working Paper, No 43.

Broadman, H.G. 2006, *Africa's Silk Road: China and India's Neil' Economic Frontier*, Washington, World Bank.

Booth, K. 1991, 'Security and Emancipation', *Review of International Studies*, vol 17.

Buzan,B. 1991, *People, States and Fear: An Agenda for International Security Studies in the Post-Cold War Era*. Boulder, CO: Lynne Reiner.

Burundi Investment Promotion Authority, 2011,General Economic Information, Newsletter.

Carbone, M. 2007, *The European Union and International Development: the Politics of Foreign Aid*, Routledge, London.

C Briceno-Garmendia and V Foster, 2010, 'Africa's Infrastructure –A Time for Transformation', Agence Française de Développement and the World Bank, The International Bank for Reconstruction and Development / The World Bank.

Chattopadhyaya, H.P. 1970, *Indians in Africa*, Calcutta, p. 333-335.

Chanana, D. 2009, 'India as an Emerging Donor', *Economic and Political Weekly*, vol. 44, no. 12.

Cheru,F. 2010, 'The Rise of China and India in Africa: What should be Africa's Response?', The Nordic Africa Institute.

CII 5th Conclave on India Africa Project Partnership, 2009, 'Celebrating Partnerships', 22 -24 March, New Delhi, India.

Cilliers, Jackie. 2004, *Human Security in Africa: A Conceptual Framework, Review* ,Monograph for the African Human Security Initiative

Collier, P. and Hoeffler, A, 2004, 'Greed and Grievance in Civil War', *Oxford Economic Papers*, 56, pp 563-595.

Conference Report on South South Cooperation India, Africa and Food Security: Between the Summits, held on 10-11 January 2011, Mumbai University http://www.mu.ac.in/arts/social_science/african_studies/ Conference%20Report,%20SSC.

Conrad, B. 2006, 'We are the Warsay of Eritrea in Diaspora: Contested Images of Eritrean-ness in Cyberspace and in Real Life' in M. Assal and L. Manger (eds),*Diasporas Within and Without Africa Dynamism, Hetereogeneity, Variation*, The Nordic Africa Institute, Uppsala, Sweden.

Damari Nyaboke Manyange, 2012, 'Converging Interests: Lessons from Counter Terrorism Strategies', in Makumi Mwagiru and Aparajita Biswas (eds) *East Africa-India Security Relations*, University of Nairobi.

Daniel D.C. Nanjira, 1976,*The Status of Aliens in East Africa*, Praeger Publishers, New York.

Desh Gupta, 1998, 'South Asians in East Africa: Achievement and Discrimination', *South Asia*, Vol. XXI, Special issue, p 128.

Dubey, A. 2010, India- Africa Relations: Historical Connections and recent Trends, in Ajay Dubey (ed) Trends in Indo- Africa Relations, Manas Publications, New Delhi.

Dubey, A. 2003, 'Indian Diaspora in the Caribbean and Africa', in Ajay Dubey (ed.), *Indian Diaspora: Global identity*, Kalinga Publications, New Delhi, pp. 127-28.

Dewitt, D. 1994, 'Common Comprehensive and Cooperative Security', Pacific Review vol. 7 no. 1, pp 2-3

Dodds K, 2007, *Geopolitics: A Very Short Introduction*, Oxford, Oxford University Press, New York.

D. Seidenberg, 1983, *Uhuru and the Kenyan Asians: The Role of a Minority Community in Kenyan Politics*, 1939-63, Vikas Publishing House, New Delhi, P. 89

East African Community (EAC), 2012, 'Draft Protocol on Peace and Security', EAC Secretariat

Economic Times, New Delhi, May 2, 2009

Export-Import Bank of India, 2006, 6 July, http://www.eximbankindia. com/ old/pressO60706.html, accessed 8 November 2008

Export-Import Bank of India, 30th Annual Report 2011-2012,

Exim Bank, 2011: 'Exim Bank's Operative Lines of Credit', Export-Import Bank of India, Mumbai.http://www.eximbankindia.com/ locstat15042011.doc [30.05.2011].

George Delf, 1963, *Asians in Uganda*, London.

Ghai, D.P. (ed), 1965, *Portrait of a Minority: Asians in East Africa* London, p. 102.

Gideon S. Wee and Derek A. Wilson, 1974, *East Africa through a Thousand Years*, London , P. 5

Gisbert Oonk, 'We Lost our Gift of Expression-Loss of the Mother Tongue among South Asians in East Africa 1880-2000', in Gijsbert Oonk (ed.),2007, *Global Indian Diasporas*, Amsterdam University Press, Amsterdam.

Global Economic Prospects 2011: Regional Annex, Sub Saharan Africa http://siteresources.worldbank.org/INTGEP/Resources/335315-

1307471336123/ 7983902-1307479336019/AFR-Annex.pdf, Accessed on 5 June 2011.

Goldstein A. et al, 2006, The Rise of China and India: What's in it for Africa? OECD, Paris.

Government of India , 2001,Report of the High Level Committee on the Indian Diaspora, ICWA, New Delhi, P .94.

Government of India, Ministry of Commerce and Industry, 2010, http:// commerce.nic.in/eidb/default.asp, accessed 176 March 2010.

Gosh, K, 2004, 'Maritime Security Challenges in South Asia and the Indian Ocean Response Strategies', Paper Presented at Center for Strategic and International Studies , January 18-20, 2004, Honolulu, Hawai.

Gregory, R. G. 1971, *India and East Africa: A History of Race Relations• within the British Empire*, 1890-1939, Oxford University Press.

Guennif S. & Ramani (eds). 2010, 'Catching Up in Pharmaceuticals: A Comparative Study of India and Brazil', United Nations University, Working Paper Series, No. 019/2010.

Gupta (ed),1971, *Indians Abroad: Asia and Africa*, Orient Longman, New Delhi P. 194

Gupta, A. 'The Asians in East Africa: Problems and Prospects,' *International Studies*, 1968-69 pp. 280-81.

Gupta, Anirudha. 1979 'India and Africa South of the Sahara', in Bimla Prasad, (ed.) *India's Foreign Policy*, New Delhi 269

Gupta, Anirudha, 'Asians in East Africa: Problems and Prospects', *International Studies* ,vol.10, July1968-April 1969, pp.270, New Delhi.

Hall, S. 'Cultural Identity and Diaspora.' in P. Williams and L. Christman(eds) 1993, *Colonial Discourse and Post-Colonial Theory. A Reader,* Harvester Wheatsheaf, New York.

High Commission of India, Nairobi, India-Kenya Relations, http://www. hcinairobi.co.ke/Pages/Kenya_india_ overview.html.

Hombara, David. 1994, Kenyan Capitalists, the State and Development, Nairobi, p. 35.

Human Security Report, 2006, *War and Peace in the 21st Century*, Oxford University Press, pp 153.

Husenchever L. and Paranhos J.2008, 'The Development of the Pharmaceutical Industry in Brazil and India: Technological Capability and Industrial Development', Economic Development Research Group, Rio di Janeiro.

IANS, 2010 'India's private sector will power Africa thrust', Vice President', 12 January, http://www.thaindian.com/newsportal/business/ indias- private-sector-will-power-a Erica-thrust-vice-president-lead_100302698html accessed on 15 February 2010.

India-Africa Summit, 2008, 'Address by Prime Minister Manmohan Singh to the first India-Africa Summit', April, http://pib.nic.in/releaseirelease. asp?relid=37177, accessed 24 February 2011.

India-Africa Forum Summit, 2008, Delhi Declaration, 09 April, New Delhi.

India Defence, 2008, Indian Navy to hold exercises with France, African Navies, 17 August.

India Today, 2011, 'Boosting ties: India offers millions but Tanzania wants more', Dar-es- Salaam', May 28.

IT Voice, 2010, 'Why Indian IT companies like TCS, Infosys and Wipro are investing in Africa', May 10.

Indian Technical and Economic Cooperation, 2010, 'About ITEC', Ministry of External Affairs, http://itec.mea.gov.in 10.12.2010.

Jackson, R,2009, 'Violent Internal Conflicts and the African States: Towards a Framework of Analysis', *Journal of Contemporary African Studies* ,20(1), pp 29-52.

Jane's Intelligence Insight , 2009 November, 'Kenya Navy'.

Jennifer G Cooke, 2011, 'Rwanda, Assessing Risk and Stability', Centre for Strategic and International Studies.

Katti et al, 2009, 'India's Development Cooperation Opportunities and Challenges' in "International Development Cooperation', Briefing Paper, No. 3, German Development Institute.

K.C. Kotecha, 1975, 'The Shortchanged: Uganda Citizenship Laws and how they were Applied to its Asian Minority', The International lawyer, Vol. 9, No.

Khadiagala,2003,'Burundi: In Dealing with Conflicts in Africa, in J Boulden, (ed), *The United Nations and Regional organizations*, Palgrave Macmillan, New York.

Kul Bhusan,1998, 'Indians in Kenya' in JK Motwani et. al. (eds.), *Global Indian Diaspora Yesterday, Today and Tomorrow*, GOPIO, New York,p 128.

Lalit Mansingh, 2009, 'Engaging a Resurgent Africa: India's Choices' in Dilip Lahiri, Jorg Schultz (eds), *Engaging with a Resurgent Africa*, Macmillan Publishers, Delhi.

Lemarchand, 1997, 'Patterns of State Collapse and Reconstruction in Central Africa: Reflections on Crisis in the Great Lakes Region', *Africa Spectrum*, vol.32, No.2.

Live Mint, Wall Street Journal, 16 February 2010, http://www.livemint. com/Companies/mMIRJi9gnndoxpUd3KOqhK/Indian-drug-makers-worried-by-East-Africa8217s-legal-prop.html, accessed on 30 November 2013.

Lugard, F.D. 1983, *Rise of our East African Empire*, London, pp.488-89.

Mangat, J.S. 1969, *A History of Asians in East Africa* c. 1886-1945, London, p.28-p140.

Macharia Munene, 2012, 'Convergence of Security Interests Kenya and India', in Makumi Mwagiru and Aparajita Biswas (eds) ,*India and East Africa Security Relations* ,IDIS and PRIASA,Nairobi.

Makrere University, 2011,'A Review of Kenyan, Ugandan and Tanzanian Public Health law relevant to Equity in Health', http://www.cehurd.org/wp-content/uploads/2011/01/Review-of-Public-Health-Laws-and-Policies-in-Kenya-Uganda-and-Tanzania.pdf

Mawdsley Emma and McCann, Gerard, 2010, 'The Elephant in the Corner? Reviewing India-Africa relations in the new Millennium', *Geography Compass*, vol. 4, no. 2, pp. 81-93.

McCann, Gerard. 2010, 'Ties that Bind or Binds that Tie? India's African Engagements and the Political Economy of Kenya,' *Review of African Political Economy*, 37/126, pp 465-482

MEA, 2012, India-Kenya Relations http://mea.gov.in/Portal/Foreign Relation/KenyaWebsiteBrief_Dec_2012-font.pdf.

MEA, 2010, Annual Report 2009-2010, New Delhi: Ministry of External Affairs.

MEA, 2011, Annual Report 2010-2011, New Delhi: Ministry of External Affairs.

Medindia, 2008, 'India Emerging as International Medical Tourism Hub', -http://www.medindia.net/news/healthwatch/India-Emerging-as-International-Medical-Tour, 22 September, accessed 11 November,

Michelle Nichols. 2010, 'Kenya says World Neglecting Somalia Security Threat,' *Mail & Guardian Online*, September 18 http://www.mg.co.za/printformat/ single/2010-0⁹

Middleton R.2008, Piracy in Somalia, www.chathamhouse.org.uk,

Mookherjee, R.K. 1957, *Indian Shipping: A History of the Sea-Borne Trade and Maritime Activity of the Indians from the Earlier Times*, Madras.

Munene Macharia. 2012,'*Geopolitics, geostrategy and the challenge of ensuring peace in East Africa*', *in 21st* Intercultural   Seminar, Nairobi.

Murphy N. M. 2007, 'Suppression of Piracy and Maritime Terrorism', *Naval War College Review,* Issue 3, pp 31

Mwambu et al, 2005, Review of Policy Options for Poverty Reduction in Kenya, Nairobi, KIPPRA, Discussion paper No. 49

Ministry of External Affairs, India, July 2005,Country Report- Tanzania, Accessed 22 October 2006, www. mea.gov.in.

Morris, H.S. 1968, *Indians in Uganda,* London, p.9.

Narlikar Amrita. 'India's Rise to Power: Where does East Africa Fit In?', *Review of African Political Economy*, 37:126,Decemebr 2010, pp 451-464

Niranjana Desai,1993, 'Asian influence in East Africa' in J.K. Motwani, Mahin Gosine and J.B. Motwani (eds), Global Indian Diaspora Yesterday, Today and Tomorrow, P. 127.

Nye, Joseph S.1966, *Pan-Africanism and East African Integration*, Harvard University Press, Cambridge.

OECD, 1989, 'Trade in Services in Developing Countries', Paris.

Okuma W & Botha A. (eds), 2007, 'Understanding Terrorism in Africa: Building bridges and Overcoming gaps', Institute of Security Studies

Oonk Gijsbert. 2006, 'Towards a Historical Explanation of the Economic Success of a Middlemen Minority', *Awaaz*, Issue III, P.8.

Osita C. Eze. 2009, 'Principal Interests of EU and India in Sub- Saharan Africa', in Dilip Lahiri, Jorg Schultz (eds) *Engaging with a Resurgent Africa*, Macmillan Publishers, Delhi.

On the Ground. 2012, 'Africa-India Trade and Investment – Playing to Strengths', Standard Chartered Bank, Global Research, 08August, pp. 110-12.

Pathak A.R. 2000, *Indo-Kenyan Cultural Ethos*, International Centre for Cultural Studies, Nagpur, P.53.

Paul Kagame. 2009, 'Why Africa Welcomes the Chinese', *Guardian*, Nov 2.

Patterson J.H. 1919, *The Man-Eaters of Tsavo and other East African Adventures*, London.

Peter Kragelund. 2010, 'India's Africa Engagement', *ARI*, 10/2010, 19 January.

Peter Kragelund. 2011, 'Back to Basics? The Rejuvenation of Non-Traditional Donors' Development Cooperation with Africa', *Development and Change* 42: 2, pp 596

P.C. Jain. 1993, 'Socio-Economic History of Indians in Kenya', in J.K. Motwani, Mahin Gosine and J.B.Motwani, (eds.), *Global Indian Diaspora Yesterday, Today and Tomorrow'* GOPIO, New York, P. 132.

P.Kragelund. 2011 'The Return of Non Dac Donors to Africa: New Prospects for African Development?', *Development Policy Review*, 26(5), pp 555-584, International Centre for Trade and Sustainable Development.

P.Sinha, 2009, 'Looking Beyond India's Development Cooperation Programme: Opportunities and threats for East Africa', Conference paper presented at "Contemporary India-East Africa: Shifting terrains of Engagements", BIEA, April 2009

Pankhust, Richard. 2002, 'Ethiopia Diaspora in India', in Richard Pankhurst (ed). *African Diaspora in the Indian Ocean*, Trenton N. J: Africa World Press

Potgieter, Thean, 2008, 'The Maritime Security Quandary in the Horn of Africa Region: Causes, Consequences and Responses', Discussion paper, East African Human Security Forum

Rao S.R. 2006,'Exim Bank: partnership in Africa's development', presentation made at the Organisation for Economic Cooperation and Development (OECD), Paris, 16-17 March.

Raja Mohan., C. 2009, 'The Remaking of Indian Foreign Policy', *International Studies*, Sage Journals January/April, vol. 46 no. 1-2,pp 147-163

Ramchandani, R.R .1976, *Uganda Asians: The End of an Enterprise*, Bombay p.90.

Rajiv Bhatia, 2010, 'Horn of Africa: Why India Should Care More,' The   Hindu,December17.http://www.thehindu.eom/opinion/lead/article959202.ace?homepage=accessed 5/30

Raman, B. 2011,'India & the Indian Ocean', Global Security News, April 7. http://global-security-news.com/2011/04/07/india-the-indian-oeean/ accessed 2/23/2012

Renu Modi, Offshore healthcare management: medical tourism between Kenya, Tanzania and India, in *India in Africa: Changing Geographies of power*.

Sharma, A. 2007, 'India and Africa: Partnership in the 21st Century', *South African Journal of International Affairs*, Vol. 14, No. 2, p. 20

Sharma, D. and Mahajan,D.2007,'Energizing Ties: The Politics of Oil', *South African Journal of International Affairs*, Vol. 14, No. 2, Winter/ Spring, pp. 37–53.

Singh, C. 1971, 'The Problems of Citizenship' in Anirudha Gupta, ed., *Indians Abroad: Asia and Africa*, New Delhi, p. 176.

Richa Nagar,1996, 'South Asian Diaspora in the Tanzania: A history retold', *Comparative studies of South Asia, Africa and The Middle East*, Vol. 16, No. 2, pp. 74-75

Robert G.Gregory, 1971, *India and East Africa: A History of Race Relations within British Empire*, 1890-1939, London, p.40.

Robert G. Gregory, 1992, *The Rise and Fall of Philanthropy in East Africa-the Asian Contribution*, Transaction Publishers, New Jersey, P. 21.

Ruchita Beri, 2008'India Woos Africa', IDSA.

Sachin Chaturvedi, Thomas Fues, Elizabeth Sidropolous (eds), 2012, *Development Cooperation and Emerging Powers*, Zed Books, London, p 177.

Sashi Tharoor. 2012, 'Familiar Lands and Uncharted Territories', *Pax Indica*, p 257 -261, Penguin Books India.

Safran, W. 1999, 'Comparing Diasporas: A Review Essay'. Diaspora, 8 (3): pp 255-291.

Schaeffer N. 2009, 'Combined Maritime Forces Works with International Navies to Counter Piracy'. Press Release, US 5th Fleet, http://www.cusnc.navy.mil/ articles/2009/089.html, accessed on 7 February 2012

Shain, Y. and Barth, A. 2003, 'Diasporas and International Relations Theory', International Organization, 57,pp 449-479.

Sheffer, G. 2003, 'Diaspora Politics: At Home Abroad', Cambridge University, Cambridge:

Shinn D. 2003, 'Terrorism in East Africa and the Horn of Africa: An Overview', *Journal of Conflict Studies*, Fall (20)

Simon Freemantle. 2010,'Indian Construction Firms making inroads into Africa',5November,   http://www.howwemadeitinafrica.com/indian-construction-firms-making-inroads-into-africa/4794/, Accessed on 2 December 2014

Simiyu, R.2008, 'Militarization of Resource Conflicts: The Case of Land Based Conflict in the Mount Elgon Region of Western Kenya', Institute of Security Studies, Pretoria.

Singh, S.2007, 'India and West Africa: a Burgeoning Relationship', Chatham House, April.

Sinha, Pranay Kumar, 2010, ' Indian Development Cooperation with Africa', in Cheru, Fantu & Obi, Cyril: *The Rise of China and India in Africa. Challenges, Opportunities and Critical Interventions*, London & New York: Zed, pp.77 – 93

Sudha Ramchandran, 2011,'India Deepens Africa Role', *Asia Times Online*, 2 June, http://www.atimes.com/ atimes/South_Asia/MF02Df01.html, accessed on 3 June 2011

Suresh Kumar, 2010, 'A perspective on Indian trade and investments in East Africa', India–Africa.

Snyder,C. 1999,'Regional Security Structures' in C, Snyder (ed). Contemporary Security and Strategy, Routledge, New York

Suri et al, 2008, 'Poverty, inequality and Income Dynamics in Kenya', 1997-2007. Tegemeo Institute , Nairobi, Working Paper Series, 30/2008

Sanjukta Bhattacharya, 2009,'India East Africa Ties', *Africa Quarterly*, Vol 49, No 1, Feb-April.

Taylor D.B. et al, 2011, 'Nutrition in Central Uganda: An Estimation of a Minimum Healthy Diet', A paper presented at the Agricultural and Applied Economics Association Annual meeting, July 21st-26th July

Taylor Ian, 22 August 2012, 'Why African presidents die abroad, SAFPI, http://www.safpi.org/news/article/2012/ian-taylor-why-african-presidents-die-abroad

Trends of Knowledge, East Africa Community, http://trends.rifanmuazin. com/East_African_Community

The Hindu, 7 March 2012 'Increase of Piracy Attacks off Somalia coast Worrisome: India', United Nations.

UNDP, Rwanda, Country Context,

http://web.undp.org/evaluation/documents/ADR/ADR_Reports/ Rwanda/ch2-ADR_Rwanda.pdf

Ullman R, 1983 'Redefining Security', *International Security* Vol. 8, No 1

V. S. Sheth, 2000, 'Dynamics of Indian Diaspora in East and South Africa', *Journal of Indian Ocean Studies*,Vol. 8, No.3, December, Pp.219-20.

Vashisht, Dinkor, 2010, 'India's Punjabi farmers investigate farming in Africa', *African Agriculture*, 26 July,

Vijay Gupta, 1964, 'Kenya's Struggle for Freedom', *Africa Quarterly*, vol.3, no.4, p.215.

Vines, Alex. 2011, 'India's Africa Engagement: Prospects for the 2011' India Africa Forum, Program paper, AFP, Chatham House, UK,

Vines, Alex and Oruitemeka, B. 2008 'India's engagement with the Africa Indian Ocean rim States', AFP briefing paper P1/08, London, Chatham House

W.T.W. Morgan, 1973, *East Africa*, London, Pp.152-53.

World Health Organisation, 'Health expenditure', World *Health Statistics*, "http://www.who.int/whosis/whostat/EN_WHS10_Part2.pdf,"http:// www.who.int/whosis/whostat/EN_WHS10_Part2.pdf, 2010,accessed 10 October 2010

WHO, 2009, 'Health workforce, Infrastructure, Essential medicines', at http://www.int/whosis/whostat/EN_WHS09_Tables6.pdf.

William Davison, 2011, 'Is Indian Investment in Ethiopian Farms a 'land grab?', *Christian Science Monitor*,23 December. http://lumilandgrab. orgipost/ view/ 1981

World Bank, 2008. 'Kenya at a glance', 24 September, http://devdata. worldbank.org/AAG/ken_aag.pdf, accessed 16 March 2012

World Bank, 2008, 'Tanzania at a glance', 24 September, http://devdata. worldbank.org/AAG/tza_aag.pdf, accessed 16 March 2012

World Bank, 2009, 'Country Brief, Kenya', January, http://www.who.int/ countries/ken/en/, accessed 16 March 2012

Yash Tandon. 'A Political Survey' in Dharam Ghai (ed), *Portrait of a Minority*, OUP, Nairobi, 1965, pp 62-65

Index

www.ingramcontent.com/pod-product-compliance
Lightning Source LLC
Chambersburg PA
CBHW030333270326
41926CB00010B/1607